I BELIEVE, NOW WHAT?

MICHAEL L. SIMPSON

I BELIEVE, NOW WHAT?

MICHAEL L. SIMPSON

Building the New Generation of Believers

COOK COMMUNICATIONS MINISTRIES
Colorado Springs, Colorado • Paris, Ontario
KINGSWAY COMMUNICATIONS LTD
Eastbourne, England

NexGen® is an imprint of
Cook Communications Ministries, Colorado Springs, CO 80918
Cook Communications, Paris, Ontario
Kingsway Communications, Eastbourne, England

First Printing, 2005
Printed in the United States of America
1 2 3 4 5 6 7 8 9 10 Printing/Year 08 07 06 05

Cover Design: Jeffrey P. Barnes
Cover Photo: © Getty Images

Library of Congress Cataloging-in-Publication Data

Simpson, Michael L., 1965-
   I believe, now what? / Michael L. Simpson.
      p. cm.
   ISBN 0-7814-4168-4 (pbk.)
   1. Christian life. 2. Theology, Doctrinal. I. Title.
   BV4501.3.S5837 2005
   248.4--dc22
                              2004026700

Dedication

Susan,
thank you for helping me answer
the most important question,
for not closing your heart,
and for opening mine more to God each day.

Can you help me answer one more?

Will you trust me to join with God to
СПАСИ и СОХРАНИ
you as long as we both shall live?

For the rest of the story,
visit www.ibelievenowwhat.com

Table of Contents

Acknowledgments

This book was born from God's ever-so-kind gift of allowing me the honor of experiencing the lives of many wonderful people and one humble dog.

Many lives inspired stories: Anya S., Connor, Galia, Ira, Jeff D., Kostya, Scott, Yanna, Ziad. Yet all inspired my own pursuit of greater intimacy with Jesus.

The original ideas for these questions came over many years from friends in three groups: Oasis in Salt Lake City, Utah, and The Verge and The Loft in Phoenix, Arizona.

This project took many paths before the correct one was revealed, and often came very close to sitting down and stubbornly refusing to step any further. I surely would have allowed it permanent rest without the brotherhood and true commitment of Mike, Quinn, Ryan, and Tedd from Open Door Fellowship; the gift of Ryan and Nols; the kindness and care of Kenneth Rundell and Natasha at Agora in St. Petersburg, Russia, where most of this work was completed. Not to mention the great mocha soy lattes at Lux coffee shop in Phoenix, Arizona, that first got it kicked into gear. (Seriously, that coffee is like a shot of pure oxygen to a late-night writer.)

My publisher, Cook Communications, once again gave me greater freedom than I deserved to explore God's leading in this project. Janet, Rich, Susan T., and others provided welcome guidance and grace.

Thanks also for the prayers of so many family and friends. Most of all, thanks to the two most important girls in my life, Susan and Maggie. I was focused and enabled by Susan's prayerful wisdom and strengthening confidence in me; and, well, Maggie just made it a whole lot of fun.

Preface

The night I prayed for Christ to become a reality to me, it was much like settling into my own bed after a long, arduous trip; curling up in a peaceful, safe, stress-free rest for the first time in … well, longer than I could remember. It felt like I was finally home. Then something of a spiritual jet lag soon set in—disrupting that so-longed-for peace. Little did I know that once I finally arrived home, the real journey would begin in earnest.

Many people share similar experiences of a new Christian life that is fraught with as much excitement as frustration. Beginning with somewhat dramatic highs and lows, they often take the wrong path—the path most traveled, the path of least resistance. The curse of wanting to do the right thing but having no idea what the right thing is can drive you to follow the greatest amount of traffic, usually leading to the camaraderie of the misdirected.

If you are like I was in those early years, what once was normal before knowing Christ now feels foreign; and what once was foreign, but should become normal, still feels kind of weird.

Man, I had questions. Do you have questions, too? This book is for the person who believes, but either just got started or feels they never got the proper footing in the Christian life.

It hopefully will help you set the proper expectations and fill in the gaps of your understanding. Are you not finding answers as quickly as you'd like? Are you not even sure exactly who to ask or what to ask for? Ignorance, failure, disappointment, and their resulting frustration can send you on a spiritual and emotional roller coaster that leaves you more sick to your stomach than excited about the next turn, but that is not the adventure God promised.

Eventually, I left that spiritual amusement park and entered the real life God intended for me all along—a life embracing the truth of my sin and my need for continual freedom. I discovered I could walk around in joy instead of feeling guilty and defeated, and I could be comfortable in my own skin if I lived spiritually unencumbered by distractions from grace. Believe me, the attraction of running one's own life is a lie and quite boring in comparison to the freedom of life with God. God promises to take you on the most exciting and rewarding journey of your life, and at the end of the day, he won't leave you broke and exhausted.

Once I burst out and stepped into the journey of lifelong grace, my skills at orienteering were honed and the ups and downs of spiritual extremes leveled a great deal. The simple mysteries of peace were unveiled, or rather, *my* blinders were removed.

I know some people who have wandered from the path of grace and never returned. Many others return, but often they have walked a great distance before realizing they've left the path—simply because they assumed it must be the right road since they had so much company along the way. Sometimes it's easier to uncomfortably travel the comfortable path, resisting the mystery of the unknown while hoping your life and relationship with God will change—yet knowing in your soul that it should be different.

Is that your experience? Sadly, it is not unique. Even with regular reading of the Bible, praying, and attending church, the landscape of life as a Christian can remain a mystery. I always wanted to know what it could or should look like, but not many people gave me practical answers. I pondered the big picture questions and wondered if others had as well. Over the years I often asked groups I taught. Friends from seventeen to fifty years old, knowing Christ from days to decades, listed questions they had about aspects of the Christian life for which they personally desired answers, questions they had trouble answering for others, and answers they found on their own but wish they had discovered earlier in their walk with Christ. Those conversations led to a series of personal discoveries and lessons taught over many years. Readers of my previous book, *Permission Evangelism*, have also requested a tool for those they have journeyed with to Christ. So, with some gentle urging from my publisher, this book was born.

Now that you've chosen to get on board this adventure, it would seem like a good idea to understand where you're going, wouldn't it? The choice to accept Christ is not just about what happens after we die—although that is the final destination. This adventure is about the freedom to live a life of joy and significance now. You don't need to miss out on the pre-heaven joy of God—a joy that transcends emotion and circumstance. It's more about getting to know your traveling Companion than your destination. This journey does not have to remain a mystery, but it will provoke many questions along the way—some with answers now, some whose answers are yet to be revealed.

So, don't sit back and hope for answers from the author as you flip these pages. Lean forward and eagerly search for truth as God's Spirit speaks through these words. Life is active, and truth fights for attention. Be quick on your feet and let's get to work on this new life of yours.

Maximizing Your Experience

You can read this book straight through; but to get the full benefit of involving God in the experience, it is recommended that you *read one chapter a day for forty days*. If the Dig Deeper section at the end of each chapter becomes too involved for you on occasion, take an extra day to ponder and pray about the topic. After a couple of days, though, try to continue with the next chapter because many of the topics complement each other and you may find clarification in unexpected places. If issues about a particular topic remain unresolved, take it up with a trusted spiritual adviser—but try to keep moving forward.

Question: The forty questions addressed in this book were selected from real conversations with real people. They are not intended to be inclusive of all questions that new and developing Christians have. Instead, they were selected to provide a base of understanding to help get you over early obstacles to fully experiencing God in your life. Don't skip over questions because you think they don't apply to you. Reading each chapter may inspire you to dig into a new area or enable you to articulate to others when you need help from someone else. You can also use this book as a reference for helping others along in their spiritual journey.

Bible Verse: The Bible can tell you everything you need to know about God. If you don't have one, get one and start reading it. The verses selected for each question are not the only applicable verses to this topic, but they will give you a representative perspective from the Bible about the topic. There are dozens of Bible versions out there including translations (from the original languages), study Bibles (with cross-referencing and notes or commentaries from scholars), devotional Bibles, and paraphrases (less literal, but often easier to understand). Unless otherwise noted, all verses in this book are from the *New International Version*.

Answer: The answer provided is *an* answer and is not inclusive of all perspectives. The answers provided are focused on speaking to the reality and practicality of life and don't represent every theological argument on the topic. Frankly, I do not believe you need to understand every theological argument on all these subjects. What you do need is to develop a desire to experience God and use the resources he provides to grow in that relationship. If you are looking for deep theological arguments, go to seminary. If you are looking for direction on how to grow in understanding and connect with God through his Word, his Spirit, the world around you, and other people—keep reading.

BOTTOM LINE
'Nuff said.

TALK TO GOD:

Developing a relationship with God that allows you to converse with him (and him with you) comfortably and naturally is absolutely the most important thing you can learn to do while walking this planet. This section is designed to introduce you to ways to relate to God; to stretch your mind to think about him in new ways; and to enable God some freedom to speak back to you through the world around you, people, the Bible and in that magical, ever-elusive thing called silence. Whatever you do, please do not skip this part each day. Spend at least five minutes in this conversation. Learn to place your focus on God and you will find answers and peace for your soul.

 # DIG DEEPER:

If you want to develop beyond just your experience of God and grow in knowledge and application of truth, take the time to dig deeper. You will find that all knowledge of God enhances your experience with God.

Beginnings

10:47 PM - December 22

Ring Ring Ring

"Hello, this is Susan. I'm not home, but please leave your name and number after the tone and I'll get back to you as soon as I can."

BEEEEEEP

"Hey, uh, Susan, this is Michael. I know it's been a long time since we've talked, but I wanted to let you know that I just prayed to accept Jesus Christ as my personal Lord and Savior. After nine months of asking questions, studying, and seeking answers, I came to the conclusion that it took too much faith to believe anything else. I just thought you should know. You've done more than any other person to point me in the right direction. Have a Merry Christmas."

7:15 AM - December 23

(one hour after morning alarm—still lying in bed)

Ohhhhh, man. What have I done?

"Hey, God, uh, this is Michael. I'm not very good at this yet, and, um, well, I don't even know if this is the right thing to say, but I've got some concerns ..."

As day two of my new life as a Christian began, I was struck with a mosaic of emotions and I was standing way too close to see the art in it. Facing fear, excitement, dread, relief, uncertainty, hope—all manner of contradictions—I wondered what was real and what was imagined. Less than nine hours earlier, my quest to prove Christianity false had ended in defeat, yet I now realized I had actually won. Sometime in the previous months that quest had evolved into a genuine desire for forgiveness and peace. Little did I know that a simple, humble, and yes, selfish prayer would warrant the adventure of a lifetime.

Once I decided that it took too much faith to believe anything else, I asked God to forgive my selfishness and be the center of this hopeless life. All manner of emotional pain and fear left me, seemingly for good. I didn't know you could actually *feel* forgiveness, but that night the conscience of my soul laid down to rest as light as the feathers in the pillow under my head. Surprisingly, I awoke the very next morning in an altogether different emotional state. It was confusing and scary, yet ripe with promise.

New questions now plagued me:

What just happened? What's the goal? Should I read the Bible? Why? How do I start? What Bible should I read? What will happen next? What do I do next? What does it mean to trust God? How do I know God's will? Who is Satan and why should I care? What kind of church is right for me? How do I find a church? What's my place in church? Who can help me? How do I explain why I'm changing? What will become of me?

Christ was finally a reality in my life, but I didn't really have a clue what that meant to my remaining days on this planet. I didn't know what I should expect from life, from God, and from myself. As the answers to my questions unfolded over time, everything about my original idea of who God was, what church was all about, and who I was to become dramatically changed. The more I learned about God and living as a follower of Christ, the more my expectations changed, and my fuzzy ideas—about everything from church to sin to grace—came into focus. Surprisingly, life actually became simpler the more I knew. Nobody's process is ever complete, mine included, but I never would have made any progress or gotten to that point without first asking some very basic questions.

Whether you've recently made a first-time decision of faith or you've recently had an experience that led you back into a committed relationship with God, this time with a new, more personal, heart perspective; you still have questions, don't you? Despite your many questions and fears, are you excited? You should be, little child of God. The gateway to the adventure of a lifetime has just been unlocked for you—it's opening day and you've got the E-Ticket to life. Don't feel embarrassed if you're having questions about God and your new life. Embrace the adventure by searching for answers. You won't find answers to all your questions between these pages, but you can at least get started, get some of those pesky ones out of the way, and get on with enjoying life with Christ.

Question 1

"What Just Happened?"

Therefore, if anyone is in Christ, he is a new creation;
the old has gone, the new has come!

2 Corinthians 5:17

So, you prayed a prayer. How do you feel? I felt like the weight of the world had just lifted off my shoulders. Something profoundly spiritual happened to me that late December 22nd evening so many years ago. Although I didn't believe in angels at the time, I actually looked up to see if there were any in my room.

Some people don't experience such a remarkable sensation, but that doesn't mean their experience is any less true.

Can you agree with the following statements?

I know God created me for a relationship with him.

Before accepting Christ, I rejected that relationship and made myself the priority in my life. I sinned—did things that were against God's desires and resulted in hurt to myself and others.

Since God is perfect and only perfection can be in his presence, my sin separated me from him; and apart from him, I am powerless to mend this relationship.

Yet God loved me so much he sent his only son, Christ, to pay the penalty for all my sin. Christ died and was raised again so that I could be in relationship with God for all eternity.

Do you desire freedom from your sin and reconciliation with God, and believe they can be had only through trust in Jesus Christ's death and resurrection on your behalf? Have you asked and believed God is capable of doing what he's promised? Yes? Then, here's what happened:

You are a new creation.

All of your past, present, and future sins were forgiven. That does not mean you won't sin again, it just means you will not be condemned for those sins.

At the moment of salvation you were given a very real gift in addition to forgiveness. Christ gave you his Spirit.

That means Christ is alive in you and serves a wonderful purpose. Christ promises that the Spirit will guide you and teach you and help you with all your decisions.

You see, your new life has begun, but the old world that you live in still exists, and your past has left a residual impact on your mind and body. You will continually change for the better if you want to, but you can't do it very well alone.

You are now in relationship with God—a very intimate relationship, the kind where he knows everything and you can feel free to share every fear, frustration, failure, hope, joy, hurt, and dream. All that is true, but you need to learn how God speaks to you and how he will work to change you.

He speaks through people, so you are called into relationships both with others who believe in Christ and with people who don't. He speaks through the Bible, so you must learn to hear him through it. He speaks directly to you, so you must learn to communicate and listen. It's just like getting to know anybody—you must spend time together.

BOTTOM LINE

The most remarkable and significant thing occurred in your life when you trusted Christ, but it was just a beginning and you will stumble quite often. Don't worry, this isn't something you have to "get right," it's something that you already are. Now you just need to figure out who that new person is, which means understanding more about God. Let's get started together—the three of us.

 TALK TO GOD:

If you prayed to receive Christ, thank God for what he did for you. If you didn't or aren't sure, now is a great time to do just that. Ask him to speak to you as you read this book and to make you aware of how he is communicating with you throughout your day.

DIG DEEPER:

Read in your Bible Romans 3:23, Romans 6:22–23, Romans 5:6–8, and John 5:24. If you do not understand how these verses apply to you, get a "Life Application" Bible and read the notes on these verses, then talk about them with someone you trust. These concepts are VERY important for you to understand in light of your new relationship with Christ.

Question 2

"What Will Happen Next?"

*Do not conform any longer to the pattern of this world,
but be transformed by the renewing of your mind. Then you
will be able to test and approve what God's will is—
his good, pleasing and perfect will.*

Romans 12:2

SHREK: For your information, there's a lot more to ogres than people think.

DONKEY: Example?

SHREK: Example? Okay, um, ogres are like onions.

DONKEY: [Sniffs] They stink?

SHREK: Yes. No!

DONKEY: They make you cry?

SHREK: No!

DONKEY: You leave them out in the sun, they get all brown, start sproutin' little white hairs.

SHREK: No! Layers! Onions have layers! Ogres have layers! Onions have layers.

You get it? We both have layers. [Sighs]
 DONKEY: Oh, you both have layers. Oh.
[Sniffs] You know, not everybody likes
onions. Cake! Everybody loves cakes! Cakes
have layers.
 SHREK: I don't care what everyone likes.
Ogres are not like cakes ... Ogres are like
onions! End of story. Bye-bye. See ya later.[1]

Donkey couldn't imagine why anyone, even an ogre, would want to be thought of as an onion. Onions are smelly. In fact, peel a single layer of an onion and it stinks rather badly. Eventually, that smell subsides, until you peel another layer. And so on, and so on, until there's no more onion left. It's just a bunch of smelly layers and each smells as bad as the last. Although they get smaller as you go, they don't stink any less.

The Christian is just like that. Sound unappealing? Well, ogres don't think so, and neither do mature Christians.

What will specifically happen *to* you I cannot say, but I can tell you what will happen *within* you. Now that you have this new heart, this new spirit living in you, a new battle has begun. The battle for your soul has been won, but the battle for your mind has just begun.

All actions, whether good or bad, begin in the mind. The new spirit in you is there to renew your mind, to change it, to make it see clearly, and then prompt it to respond appropriately. We all grow up believing lies about ourselves, about God, and about other people. These lies took root many years ago and have since sprouted and borne whatever dark fruit they produce. As an example, if you believed that joy and happiness in your life were dependent on what others thought of you, the fruit of that bad seed likely manifested itself as a never-ending need to please others by changing yourself to suit them.

The lies you believe lead to the lies you live. But Christ said he is the way, the truth, and the life. He's truth, and with his Spirit residing in your heart, you now have truth within you. The battle inside, therefore, is between truth and lies. There is no great "truth nuclear weapon" that will wipe out the enemy all at once—which is good, since immediate destruction of the lies so deeply rooted within your idea of yourself might actually destroy *you*. So one by one, the enemy is sought after, revealed, and destroyed in hand-to-hand combat.

All of those lies you believed throughout your life— whether from childhood experiences, the media, or spiritual influence—must be rooted out one at a time. Just like peeling the layers of an onion, every time a new lie is revealed you want to turn your head. But that response is also a lie. Sure, sin is bad, but the Holy Spirit within you reveals sin as proof that God loves you and wants you close. He reveals it so that you can deal with it together, trusting in God to change you in the process.

BOTTOM LINE

You will not know the details of how your life will unfold, but the details of your heart must be revealed and understood for you to find joy and peace. God has started on that process already. If you feel sad when you sin and run *to* God, that's from God. If you feel condemned, that's your past self lying to you again to lead you *away* from God—to convince you that God doesn't love you anymore, or you aren't worthy of his love. You must remember that God reveals the sin so you can know him better by trusting him to change you, heal you, and free you. This process never ends. Embrace it with joy or live a life of defeat. I, for one, prefer victory and joy.

TALK TO GOD:

Pray for God to reveal what he desires to change in you. Thank God for the Holy Spirit and the conviction that comes from knowing him. Thank him for not condemning you, but for revealing your sin to free you from it. Ask him to show you the next step and embrace it even if it makes you uncomfortable.

DIG DEEPER:

Pray for understanding from God's Spirit. Then read John 16:5–15 and write down what you think the Holy Spirit is telling you about his role in your life.

Question 3

"What's My Next Step?"

*"Ask and it will be given to you; seek and you will find; knock
and the door will be opened to you. For everyone who asks
receives; he who seeks finds; and to him who knocks, the door will
be opened."*

Matthew 7:7–8

Faith begins today. Faith will begin again tomorrow, and the
next day, and the next. God will continually call you into situations that require you to choose to trust completely in him or
to trust in yourself or others. How you choose to face the circumstances of life—with or without faith—will either tear you
apart or hold you together.

Have you ever watched an artist at work? They start with
a few lines or a couple of blobs of paint on paper or canvas
that make sense only to the artist. The completed work is
already in the artist's mind but only he can see it. With each

stroke of pencil or brush, more details emerge. But until the work is finished, you can't be totally sure what the artist has in mind—he may surprise you. God, the master artist, wants you to stand and watch as he paints his own portrait in your life. Every decision, moment, lie, fear, or hope that you entrust to him is another brushstroke across the canvas. Little by little, his face becomes clear. As the form takes shape, his ever-so-soft eyes will pierce your heart and his strong hands will invite you into the frame.

There is a great deal you do not know today. That will continue to be true throughout your life because you are in relationship with a God who is infinitely more than you can ever fully grasp. But really, would you want it any other way? Knowing that as long as you live on this planet there will be more to discover about God and yourself keeps life exciting.

God does not expect you to be superhuman; that's his job. Even building your faith is his job, but you must allow that to occur. It happens a little at a time with each daily choice to trust. Life is just full of surprises, so since God doesn't give you a crystal ball to look into the future, you're gonna get cold-cocked now and then and not know what the heck to do—just like before you knew Christ. The difference now is that you have something to trust in, somewhere to go, and someone to rely on. That thing, that place, that person is God and his character.

Your next step is to do the thing that will best help you to know God: trust him with your uncomfortable places. If you are anxious about something right now, that may very well be where God is choosing to reveal more of himself to you. You must enter that place or remain anxious.

If you haven't already done so, you need to tell someone

who has a healthy relationship with God about your decision to follow Christ. Then you need to ask for help. "But wait, you said I needed to have faith in God." Yes, and this is where it begins. You need to admit your ignorance and need, let go of your pride and say, "I don't know much about God and the Bible, and I need someone to teach me."

BOTTOM LINE

You took a really big step when you chose to believe Christ can change your present and future, and now it is time to practice walking. Ask God to lead you to a person who can help. Start reading the Bible and ask God to help you understand what he wants to tell you. Above all, if you have a question—*ASK.* If you have a concern—*ASK.* But keep moving forward. Knocking on doors is an action that takes personal initiative. It requires faith that whoever is on the other side is good and will welcome you. It's okay. God's waiting for you and he's got dinner warming.

 TALK TO GOD:

Ask God to reveal to you anything that might be in the way of trusting him. Talk to him about what is at the root of that fear and how to get past it.

 DIG DEEPER:

Write down the story of how your perspective of God has changed over the years and how you would like it to change in the future.

Question 4

"How Do I Know That Anything Happened?"

That if you confess with your mouth, "Jesus is Lord," and believe in your heart that God raised him from the dead, you will be saved. For it is with your heart that you believe and are justified, and it is with your mouth that you confess and are saved.

Romans 10:9–10

No one has ever seen God; but if we love one another, God lives in us and his love is made complete in us. We know that we live in him and he in us, because he has given us of his Spirit. And we have seen and testify that the Father has sent his Son to be the Savior of the world. If anyone acknowledges that Jesus is the Son of God, God lives in him and he in God. And so we know and rely on the love God has for us. God is love. Whoever lives in love lives in God, and God in him. In this way, love is made complete among us so that we will have confidence on the day of judgment, because in this world we are like him.

1 John 4:12–17

"How can somebody know if they don't have a specific date, time, or some remarkable spiritual experience?"

"I prayed and believed. I was told that was all you needed to be saved, but how can I be sure?"

"I don't feel any different or look any different; and I sure don't seem to act much different."

"I thought at the time that it was real, but even just a few days later I started to wonder."

"Can I really know?"

Have you ever rolled over in the morning with a head full of pillow down and wondered if what your fuzzy memory recalled as having happened the night before was a dream or reality? Everyone goes through times of questioning what's real and what's not. Perhaps you're thinking that about your salvation experience. You aren't the first! In fact, I actually hope you do question it, for a couple of reasons.

First, the fact that you are questioning your salvation may very well affirm that you have truly made a decision to follow God. That may not seem logical, but let me explain: If there is a spiritual world that desires to keep every person from resting in God's grace (there is, by the way), those evil forces do not give up once a person makes the decision to trust Christ. The best enemy tactic to undermine your future is to convince you that nothing happened, then steer you back to your old life, and get you to deny any attempts for real change. So if your relationship with God is attacked in any way, it's probably because your relationship *is* real. Otherwise Satan wouldn't really care, now would he?

That's not the best reason, and probably something that just a few of you needed to hear, but the other reason I hope you really dig into whether you are saved or not is because believers who question their salvation usually come out on the other side with a deeper understanding of their need for God's love and his inexhaustible supply. God is not afraid or offended by our questions. In fact, he encourages them, so the decision you made to follow God is a great place to start. The truth is, if you don't question it, somebody else will.

I once prided myself on preying upon the unsuspecting Christians trying to evangelize me. These encounters were disastrous for those who had never really analyzed their own decision. A few well-placed questions such as "Without using Bible verses, tell me the impact God has had on your life," and a few "How can you *really know*?" questions and scientific theories presented as facts were all that was usually needed to rattle their stances. Many times they left my presence in tears, questioning their own salvation as I sat wallowing in smug approval, watching them scurry away in fear and confusion. Look out for those like the old me. They're out there: the angry, well-read guy in the office; the young girl hurt by a church leader; the voice in your head whispering, "Nothing has changed."

Fortunately, knowing *is* possible and required, so you can get on with the business of life. I remember the first time I installed a computer network, not really having a clue what I was doing. I installed all the network cards, plugged in the cables and computers, loaded the cryptic software—just following the instructions, actually—and then held my breath when the first PC tried to connect.

It worked, but there was this sense that it would all fall apart any minute. Nevertheless, I had to assume it was working and was good enough for what I needed or nothing would ever get accomplished. One more computer installed, then another, then another—until everything was talking, files and printers and information shared seamlessly. The technology of it was still a bit of a mystery to me, but months later, it was still chugging along. After that successful experience, I never questioned another installation and was able to focus on more important aspects of the technology. The installation was a basic "given" and the real work began afterward. So it is with Christ.

There isn't a "right" way to accept Christ. You can pray with someone; follow a document point by point; read a book; see a verse and know it is true; pray alone in your home, car, hotel room, airplane; or pray along with a TV show. The "how" makes no difference at all. I know someone who can only track her acceptance of the truth of Christ to a vague recollection of hearing a popular rock song on the radio in her bedroom. In that moment, she just knew that Jesus was true and real—and that she would never be the same.

Just last month, a radiant young girl named Anya who had attended Bible studies for over two years began to cry in church one Sunday. She cried again at a park that afternoon, then during a pool party, on the way home, throughout the night, and into the next day. When I asked her if her tears were happy or sad, she said they were happy. The next day when her close friend said, "You don't need to make a decision until you get your most important questions answered about Jesus," Anya replied, "I don't think I have any more questions. I believe and I think it happened yesterday." Instead of needing a prayer of salvation, Anya was ready to pray a definitive prayer thanking God for Jesus dying for her and giving her his Spirit. She knew it was done.

If anyone ever says, "You didn't do it this way or that, so you aren't saved," feel free to ignore them, *if* you can rely on these two tests:

Did you follow the instructions?

Did it work?

The instructions simply say that you first really need to believe that Jesus died for your sins and was raised from the dead. Do you? Well, that puts you in the same position of Satan. He believes that Jesus died for your sins and was raised from the dead, too—but he will not call him Lord. Calling Jesus Lord means that you desire to put him in a position of authority in your life—the ultimate authority. Saying it—out loud—makes all the difference. But belief without action is worth absolutely nothing and can actually be dangerous.

If you were standing on a railroad track and saw a train barreling toward you and you had complete intellectual understanding and acceptance that stepping off the tracks would save your life but refused to act on that understanding, you would be guaranteed death. Belief means nothing without acting on that belief. If you believe but can't say it out loud, there's probably still something inside you that doesn't want to let go of control. Stop now and figure out what that is and then we'll keep talking.

But if you have both believed with your heart and confessed with your mouth, there is another action for that faith that proves your salvation. No, it's not what you "do" for your church, or "do" differently by acting like a more moral person. Most people can change their behavior if they want to. That doesn't necessarily require God's Spirit at all. The difference isn't what you *do* but what you *are*. You don't have to feel or look different to yourself straight away, because sometimes change happens slowly, but eventually some of these questions should ring true for you:

Do you feel guilty for something that once felt normal? That's God's Spirit saying he wants to free you from something that's hurting you.

Do you hurt for somebody else? Do you hurt for strangers? That's God's heart molding yours into his image.

Do you want to tell people about God? That's God's passion infecting you.

Do you find that when you read the Bible, it looks different or makes more sense? That's God's Word coming alive through interpretation of the Spirit in you.

Does it frustrate you that others don't see what you see? Are friends or family treating you differently? That's God's truth shining through you into the darkness.

Are there new emotions in you, however confusing they may be? That's the new creation that is you, trying to break through the caked-on crud of many years in prison.

Do you ever have the urge to do the right thing, even when you still don't act on it? That's your new life pushing through the ground.

Do you desire to give to others what they don't deserve, whether a good word, gentle touch, helpful finances—or, conversely, to stop giving hurtful words, harsh touches, or punishing debt? Are you becoming more empathetic to the needs of others? That's love—the source of which is God. He doesn't "teach" love—he IS love. If you have it growing in you, be assured of your salvation.

Even if these last proofs aren't so evident to you yet, they probably are to others. Give it some time. Don't be in such a hurry to radically change and don't try to force it. In due time, if you believe and confess and trust, it will all come. Truth is truth. God's promise is real. Maybe that's your second step of faith.

BOTTOM LINE
Doubts aren't a huge problem because they can never change what is true. They only become a problem when you give them power to lead you away from truth. Continue to trust in the life-changing death and resurrection of Jesus Christ and changes will come a little at a time, if you desire these changes and pray for God to move you in that direction. That is a promise. That is God's promise. If he said it, it is so. Will you choose to trust that as well?

 TALK TO GOD:

Thank God for your salvation and tell him what you think about it. Ask him to reveal other parts of your life where he would like to give you new freedom.

 DIG DEEPER:

Make a list of what you believe God has done for you. When others who know your "before" and "after" talk about how you've changed, write down their comments. Ask God to show you if those are the changes he wants for you.

Question 5

"Will I Be Happy?"

*I have set the Lord always before me. Because he is at
my right hand, I will not be shaken. Therefore my heart is glad
and my tongue rejoices; my body also will rest secure,
because you will not abandon me to the grave,
nor will you let your Holy One see decay.*

Psalm 16:8–10

Today, as I escape to my computer to pen these thoughts, I'm saddened and broken inside. This pain cannot be blamed on my morning coffee with the *New York Times*, whose pages are rife with stories of deadly battles around the world, gross editorial misrepresentations of Christianity and biblical truth, or the legal system's support for the moral decline of our society. The pain cannot even be blamed on the conversation I had last night with several family members about terribly disturbing news that has created much pain, damaging trust and hope between loved ones. It isn't due to the stillborn baby my dear friends delivered last week, or the news yesterday that a long time colleague and all-around great guy suddenly died, leaving a wife and twin boys alone and fatherless. It's been quite a week, but I don't blame them. No, this pain is God's fault.

That likely strikes you as odd and possibly more than a little disturbing, especially considering the heading under which these words reside. Am I angry at God? Not in the slightest. Am I resentful? Not for many, many years. No, today I am mature. Tomorrow I may act more childlike spiritually, although I pray I won't, but today I am sobered with the heart of God. Today I not only see this world's loneliness and darkness as God sees it, albeit from my comparatively limited view, but I also celebrate my Lord, and that makes me smile.

Don't get me wrong, I am terribly sad today. I physically hurt inside from the pain of others, but I see this as a gift from my loving Father. This sadness is not the destination; it is, though, a needed transport for the welcome arrival of the goal of spiritual maturity. Selfishness and pride once insulated me from the pain of others, but Christ changed all that and awakened compassion.

Sadness does not define your growth or make you spiritually mature, just as happiness cannot—nor can any emotion for that matter. What defines your spiritual maturity at any given moment is *what isn't moved* more than *what moves you*. What isn't shaken in the storm of life's trauma? What isn't blown by the wind of conviction? What doesn't budge under the strain of praise and success?

Sitting today at lunch with my close friend and confidant, Scott, I shared my week and told him about the choice to fast today so as to drink deeply of this sadness. A fast is certainly a strange thing to announce at a lunch meeting, but the day was prescheduled and I valued time with Scott more than food. As expected, he desired to cheer me up, but I halted his attempt. This day should be sad, and I fasted as to not miss anything, to heighten awareness, and to remind me to pray with each pang of hunger. I explained how in my sadness I still celebrated God, because regardless of these distressful circumstances, they did not change the reality of who I am or the reality of the character, power, and love that I have come to know of my Lord. They did not move. These truths through today's testing are found firm, unshakable, and quite real.

The wonder of life, the essence of true God-given joy, is found in this knowing—peace despite circumstance, hope regardless of difficulty, truth challenged and not found wanting. I know God is in control and that he will allow even the bad stuff that happens in life to be used for good. Bad things don't stop being bad, but they can't ultimately defeat us. Peace can be had in sadness as much as in happiness, with neither avoided or held too firmly. More specifically, the promise from Christ of the gift of God's Holy Spirit is exactly that. This gift of the Christian life in no way defines the circumstances that will come your way. You are not promised a life of ease or discomfort, financial freedom or poverty, avoidance of death or illness, or even happiness or sadness. You are not promised that *life* will be different, but you are assured that your *living* can change.

Does this sadden you? Are you depressed because this doesn't meet your expectations? Had you hoped that the Christian life would make all your pain disappear and justice would be on your side now that the power of Christ is in your corner?

If so, take heart. Don't let a bit of sobering reality deter you from an amazing life of hope and genuine peace. Within the difficulties of life, more so than the celebrations, you discover your greatest need for God, and that's where joy is found—in the knowledge of the goodness, love, and power of your Creator and Savior. This is not a description of an elite group of spiritual superheroes. This is what you were made for. This is the *normal* Christian life!

There is quite a huge difference between joy and happiness. Happiness is a feeling, and feelings come and go. You will be happy as a Christian, but being a Christian does not guarantee your happiness because God has not yet chosen to extract you from this world. Life still goes on—at times *with* you, other times *at* you. Sometimes you should be sad, and I hope more often than not you will find happiness. Joy and peace, though, can exist in the midst of all if you seek a greater understanding of God.

BOTTOM LINE

Yes, you will be happy, probably more so than ever, but don't stop there. Life with God offers oh so much more. Set your sights higher than emotions. Seek truth. Seek God. Ask "who" is God, not "why" he chooses to allow bad things to occur, and you will receive answers.

TALK TO GOD:

Thank God for his wisdom and ask him to help you understand and trust it more. Is there something that makes you sad? If so, ask God to show you how to delight in him in the midst of the sadness.

 DIG DEEPER:

Some Bibles have a concordance in the back that allows you to look up verses by keywords. Use the concordance and search for verses on *joy*. Or check out http://bible.gospelcom.net/bible and use the keyword *joy* to search for verses. Write at least one verse down that feels familiar in your heart or stirs a longing or desire in you.

Question 6

"What Do I Need Now?"

We have much to say about this, but it is hard to explain because you are slow to learn. In fact, though by this time you ought to be teachers, you need someone to teach you the elementary truths of God's word all over again. You need milk, not solid food! Anyone who lives on milk, being still an infant, is not acquainted with the teaching about righteousness. But solid food is for the mature, who by constant use have trained themselves to distinguish good from evil.

Hebrews 5:11–14

Your entire life has been a lie, a farce, a facade of escape and pursuit of comfort, and a denial of truth. But now you have chosen truth at all cost. You know that truth often hurts, but it is always a better path in the long run. You are tired of lies. You are sick of hurting yourself and others. You want freedom.

You want to live a life that is honoring to God. You understand your need and you turned over your life to the Creator of the Universe.

This is the first step of your new life. What you lack in experience you may initially make up for in enthusiasm. You may not be trained to recognize needs and ask for help as well as recovering addicts do, but you had better start thinking like they do. You must get help to break old patterns in your life, and the knowledge of your risk gives you a sober (pardon the pun) expectation that it will be difficult. You must get a list of people to go to in times of temptation, doubt, or even joy. You must start sharing these emotions and experiences with fellow believers as soon as you can, because if you don't, it will become increasingly difficult in time. There is a comfortable vulnerability that lingers from the first smell of grace shortly after accepting Christ, but it will fade if not nurtured.

Search high and low for someone to walk with you in that first year. Meeting and studying with a mature believer one-on-one or in a group of two or three for one year will catapult your spiritual development ahead. This is the most critical time of your development because it is your most vulnerable time. Take your spiritual maturity as seriously as a former addict who desperately desires to live a sober life, and be willing to do anything to allow that to become a reality.

Don't be in such a hurry to serve and get involved in church activities. Early on, it is fine to think a little selfishly, because you need to get a good handle on this new person called you. It is okay to say no, or not yet, but be open to God's leading. If you volunteer for something, make sure you do it with joy and not a sense of obligation. If you do it, make sure you do it for God and not just for the desire to fit into the community. You will be taking, probably for the first time, an honest look at your life—past, present, and future. This is serious business and it takes time. Do not assume that it will "just happen." Your big milestones will be thirty, sixty, ninety days and one year. If you invest your whole heart into discovering who God is and who you now are as a follower of Jesus Christ, the dividends will pay off for the rest of your life.

One great way to start sorting this out, getting a proper perspective, and celebrating the value of community is to tell your story. There's no right or wrong to how you do this, but it is critical to accepting and understanding what has occurred. Start with a person who was involved in your process of discovering Christ, then try to talk to a group of believers, maybe eventually your whole church. What you will learn about God as you outline your story and answer the questions people ask will cement your decision and positively impact many other people. You will begin to see God at work through you and I guarantee that you will learn to crave more and more of him—*especially* if thinking of doing this scares you stiff.

You will also begin to develop a love of his Word, which is the most critical step to spiritual maturity. All the answers to life and freedom are in that book, if you can just learn to discern the leading of the Holy Spirit when reading and studying it. Everything you will ever want to know about yourself, God, and life will somehow connect to your experience in that book. If you focus your efforts there and then act on the changes that occur in you, all things are possible.

BOTTOM LINE
You were changed the moment you trusted Christ with your past, present, and future. Now it is time to heal and help others

find healing. Your priority is your spiritual development, which is learning to discern God's voice, to understand his Word, and to act on the changes that are occurring in you. God will bring you people to help, but it is up to you to take advantage of those resources. Don't get distracted by acting like a Christian. Don't settle for being changed—become remarkable!

 TALK TO GOD:

Thank God for creating you—for *rebirthing* you as a person with a brand-new, perfectly clean heart. Acknowledge that he can change and mature you if you choose to allow that. Ask him to help you make your spiritual maturity a priority. Tell God that you give him freedom to do whatever he wants to you so that he will become your priority (It can be a scary prayer if you really mean it—but trust in God's goodness and it will be okay).

DIG DEEPER:

Go to a park or playground and spend some time observing children from a year old and up. Observe how children stretch the boundaries of their limitations as they try to speak, walk, run, climb, or just sit up. Watch how most children get up when they fall and try again. Think about parallels to your spiritual development. Think about the aspects of children that lead them into maturity and choose to emulate those. Are you curious about God? Are you willing to take the hand of someone older who is willing to support and guide you? How aware of your own limitations and abilities are you? Are you tempted to try to walk or run before you have learned to crawl? Can you be content with today's discoveries, knowing that tomorrow will hold more?

Question 7

"Will God Hurt Me?"

"For I know the plans I have for you," declares the Lord,
"plans to prosper you and not to harm you,
plans to give you hope and a future."

Jeremiah 29:11

Stern discipline awaits him who leaves the path;
he who hates correction will die.

Proverbs 15:10

One of my greatest joys while living in Arizona was running through the desert mountains with my dog, Maggie. Quite the enthusiastic athlete, she would run until she dropped unless I kept a close watch. One day, I wasn't as vigilant as usual. She is a great runner, but the heat can be taxing when you run in a fur coat. Even when she was tired, Maggie still kept up really well while running right behind me. So I became accustomed to an occasional tired tug on the leash towards the end of a run.

This day, though, about six or seven miles into our run (where we both tend to get a bit tired in the heat of the desert) the leash was a little more taut, requiring me to pull her along a bit and bark out encouragement: "Only two miles to go, Maggie, keep it up." Some may think this ridiculous, but like any good dog owner, I assume my dog understands even the most complex or obscure communication. *Dog and owner* is a logic-free relationship.

When no encouragement helped, I stopped to see if she was all right. To my shock and horror, she had a softball-sized chunk of cactus sticking out of her right shoulder. It was one of those nasty little cacti with hundreds of tiny needles per square inch that break apart and grab you when you're within striking distance. She must have stepped off the trail to sniff something. The tugging on the leash was from her biting at her shoulder while we ran, leaving fifty or more cactus needles in her lips, tongue, and gums. She never whined or tried to stop running. She just pushed on, trying to please me, struggling through her pain. I guess she thought I preferred her running to asking for help.

I know a lot of Christians like that, and I've been that way myself on occasion—running along behind my Master, trying to please him, ignoring my pain, but running the race slower and slower, dreading the next step as if he preferred it that way. Fortunately, that day God gave me a life picture of his love that will stay with me and forever alter my response to pain or need.

The only way my dear little Maggie could carry on and be healthy was to submit to what she least desired but most needed. I took off my shirt, wrapped it around my hand, laid her on her left side, and tried to pull the cactus off. She predictably yelped, jumped up, and tried to get out of my reach. The man she trusted and loved was hurting her. She was suddenly not just in pain, but also confused, scared, and seeking escape. It was as if she was thinking, *Living with the pain is easier. In time it will be all right. I can deal with it on my own.*

As her master, I knew better. I pulled her close, spoke calming words of assurance so she would relax, laid her gently down again, and eased down next to her. Then I threw one leg over her haunches and my left arm across her neck so no amount of struggling would free her from my grip. Her eyes filled with fear as I grabbed the cactus and yanked. One big yelp and she was released from my grip.

Suddenly she realized it didn't hurt as badly to walk and she came to my side wagging her tail, thinking it was all done. Again, I knew better. After a few moments, when she was ready, I laid her down again; pulled out my needle-nosed pliers (I've lived in the desert for awhile so I was prepared); and started plucking the needles from her shoulder, then her face, and finally her gums. At first, Maggie struggled just as before, but soon she realized that even though the pain I inflicted was sharp, it was temporary, and with each pluck she was freed from deeper pain.

As she began to succumb to her knowledge of her master's character and relinquish fear to trust, she laid down, wincing, but at peace—staring deep into my eyes just to make sure that they never stopped speaking love.

God showed me something of my own soul and the soul of all humanity that day. Our Master desperately wants to free us from the pain caused by our own missteps in life when we stray from the path set before us. Learning to trust can hurt because it is fraught with the unknown. Fortunately, it gets easier as we learn to trust in the character of our Master.

BOTTOM LINE

Yes, God will hurt you, but he will never harm you. Although the pain you receive at the hands of God will confuse you, frustrate you, and probably make you cry, the character of God and his promises never change. If you believe he is good, he can't be bad. If you believe he is love, he can't be hate. God is incapable of contradicting his nature. He won't change, so you must figure out who he really is to make sense of difficult times. Seek God in pain to find purpose in it. Trust in what you know from personal experience, and trust in what the Bible says when you doubt. Through time, as you choose to live by faith in God's character and love, those two will align.

TALK TO GOD:

Thank God for his great love that leads him to allow temporary pain when it ultimately is for your benefit. Ask for the faith and trust to appreciate his strong love, as well as his gentle love.

 ## DIG DEEPER:

Think about and write down what would happen to children if they were never disciplined. Now draw parallels to your relationship with God and how discipline can benefit you.

Question 8

"Will I Become One of THEM?"

≋

"A new command I give you: Love one another. As I have loved you, so you must love one another. By this all men will know that you are my disciples, if you love one another."

John 13:34–35

Maybe it was a commitment problem—a commitment to be what I had always rejected as an atheist. The night I accepted Christ was fantastic … the best. But the first morning after, I was freaking out. I was torn between the fear of transforming into one of those "Christian freaks" I had loathed all of my life, or living a life without peace if I didn't have Christ. Which was worse?

I knew from my unquenchable desire for peace, truth, forgiveness, genuine joy, and change (surprisingly, care for my eternity wasn't even factoring into the equation at this point), I needed to follow Christ. But I dreaded the idea of Borg-like conformity, boredom, prejudice, and judgment of my fellow man—all those stereotypes that comprised my twisted picture of the "official" Christian life.

So, for the second time in as many days, I prayed—this time a little differently:

"Lord, please, please, never let me forget what it is like to live a life without you, so that I will always be able to relate to those that do. Amen."

That was a nice way of saying, "Lord, please don't let me become a freak."

I truly believe that one of the key influences that kept me from pursuing Christ was *Christians*—well, at least people who claimed to be Christian. To be fair, 84.2 percent of Americans claim to be Christian[2], but statistically over 60 percent of them don't agree with the basic foundations of biblical truth. Someone simply claiming to be a Christian has little bearing on whether or not he has a relationship with God through faith in Jesus Christ, or that he even has the slightest clue what that means. In America, a nation founded by dedicated Christ followers, the label "Christian" has become the lazy man's moniker for those who have yet to choose to commit to any belief system.

I once met a man who was deeply hurt in a church and consequently swore off all religion. He was an angry, bitter man who searched out arguments in the local coffeehouse with anyone who was brave enough to read their Bible in public. I was sad for him, and although I refused to enter into his arguments, I left him with something to think about one day.

As I got up to leave, I turned and asked him, "Have you ever had a lemon car before? One that really was a piece of junk and caused you a lot of trouble?"

"Sure, why?"

"Was it the car you drove up in today? The car over there?"

"No, I got rid of that car a long time ago."

"Oh, so *cars* weren't the problem. It was *that particular car*, right?"

And I turned and left him to think about his "one of those" mentality.

During my initial search for truth, I was fortunate and found a group of true Christians at a wonderful church. When I relocated far away, I stumbled upon a not-so-wonderful place, but fortunately I didn't give up there. Since then, I have found the beauty of God's loving bride (the church) throughout America, Africa, England, Scotland, Wales, Russia, France—hundreds of places. Sure, some of them are a little tight in their wedding dresses, and some have some pretty wacky hairdos, but they feel beautiful because they know their groom and are living in his love. And if that's enough for him, that's enough for me.

BOTTOM LINE

That fear of yours—the one that rears up while you are watching the news or reading the paper about people carrying signs claiming how God hates one people group or another, the one that encourages you to disassociate yourself from community—it's another of those lies. Just as God created you to be beautiful in your spirit, his bride, the church, may not be perfect; but her spirit is and he desperately loves her. Don't let one bad experience keep you from identifying with his bride. Don't let a heart of judgment keep you from experiencing the love of community you were called to be a part of. Keep looking until you see what God sees.

 TALK TO GOD:

Thank God for the gift of his Spirit of love in you and in all believers who trust him. Ask him to develop a heart for loving others in you. Ask him how you can love another believer very practically. Be still. Listen. Write down what comes to mind.

 DIG DEEPER:

Read 1 Corinthians 13:1–7 and assess your own ability to love compared to these verses.

Question 9

"How Does God Communicate?"

*The Lord said, Go out and stand on the mountain in
the presence of the Lord, for the Lord is about to pass by.*

*Then a great and powerful wind tore the mountains apart and
shattered the rocks before the Lord, but the Lord was not in the
wind. After the wind there was an earthquake, but the Lord was
not in the earthquake. After the earthquake came a fire, but the
Lord was not in the fire. And after the fire came a gentle whisper.
When Elijah heard it, he pulled his cloak over his face and went
out and stood at the mouth of the cave.*

1 Kings 19:11–13

Have you ever stood on the edge of the Grand Canyon? Have
you ever watched endless waves pound the seashore? Have
you ever sat quietly, completely alone in a meadow or woods,
to just listen? In these moments you sense you aren't alone at

all, that there's something greater than you and me. It's God and he's speaking directly to you. Everything ever created or that ever will be created, even you, can reveal truth about the Ultimate Creator.

Rocks, mountains, wind, trees, animals—all speak of God's wisdom and power. As the creator of mankind, he also speaks through every action and creation of ours. Words, music, literature, and art can all act as his tools of communication when he so desires. Before you knew God personally, these things were used to woo you into that relationship, to urge you to ask questions, to stir desire for more within your soul. Eventually, when you were ready, that voice led you to discover those answers and now you find yourself in a new place with new ears.

Now, since you have God's voice guiding and teaching you through his Spirit inside, your depth of understanding can dramatically increase. Average, rather mundane moments of your day can be messages from God if translated by that spiritual voice within, but you must listen. This usually means that every now and then you must stop your mind, your body, and the parts of your world that you can control to seek God, asking him to reveal himself.

As you listen, it is often difficult to discern one voice from the other:

"You should take the job."

"It's okay to ask her out."

"God doesn't think that about you."

"What could it hurt to do it just once?"

"That's wrong. Don't do it."

To learn to distinguish his voice from your own or the ever-present forces that desire to drown him out, you must go directly to the source. In the heat of the moment, with just the situation and a feeling to guide you, you'll get it wrong a lot. But if you check the thing you heard, or at least feel you heard, against what the Bible says, you will find either contradiction or agreement. The loud voice grabs your attention, but as you stop to read and seek confirmation in prayer, the verses and that voice of translation will guide you. Simply ask for truth to be revealed; use the concordance at the back of your Bible to search for verses that address the topic at hand and believe God chooses to communicate this way to you.

BOTTOM LINE

Just as in any relationship, the more time you spend with God, the more easily you will recognize the tone and timbre of his voice and the better able you will be to test all voices to know if they are from God. If a desire within you seems to contradict what you know about God and his character or you don't understand what the Bible says, seek counsel from somebody who knows God and demonstrates wisdom in his or her own life. *"Is this from God or from me?"* is always an appropriate question to ask. In addition, use the Spirit as your guide as you look and listen for what God is communicating through circumstances, his creation, the Bible, and people.

TALK TO GOD:

Find a very quiet, peaceful place. Sit with your eyes open and tell God everything you have on your mind—out loud. Talk to God like he is sitting right there with you. Be quiet. Sit still long after it feels uncomfortable. Listening is an important part of communicating with God. After a while, write down any thoughts in your head.

 # DIG DEEPER:

Over the next few days, practice actively listening for how God might be communicating with you. Pray for guidance, read verses associated with the topic (again, using a concordance or the Internet), and look for any "coincidences" throughout your days that relate to the topic you talked to God about. Record all these events and talk to someone who is close to God and whom you trust about their perspective on these occurrences.

Question 10

"What Does a Healthy Relationship with God Look Like?"

"Let us rejoice and be glad and give him glory! For the wedding of the Lamb has come, and his bride has made herself ready. Fine linen, bright and clean, was given her to wear."

Revelation 19:7–8

The bride, having spent all day being pampered by family and friends and feeling more beautiful than at any time in her life, pauses at the back of the chapel as beautiful music announces her arrival to all in attendance. At first glance the groom's knees buckle slightly and he can't contain his amazement at how gorgeous she is, how fortunate he feels, and how honored he is. The multitudes stand and turn with the sound of oohs and ahhs punctuating the organ music. Those celebrating this blessed event wipe away tears of joy as they fondly reflect on their own marriage or hope for the same in their future.

Oh, how beautiful she feels; how loved; how special. The procession slowly makes its way down the aisle and finally there she is, standing face to face with her life partner. Both bride and groom are caught up in the moment. No thoughts of the future; no fears; just peace and joy, staring into each other's eyes, basking in the magic of the day.

Imagine what the groom feels, or the bride feels, and what the people in attendance are experiencing. This is how God feels about *you*. He's that groom with incredible longing in his eyes and you're that beautiful bride, totally accepted, adored, and honored. The angels in heaven and the true believers on earth sing and dance as you take the hand of your lover. God chose this picture over all other relationships to let you know how he feels for you today, tomorrow, and forever.

God created us for a relationship and he says it looks like a marriage. He desires us to picture in our heads probably the most romantic, exciting, magical moment of any marriage— the wedding day. He claims the role of the groom and calls us his bride.

Yes, this marriage thing certainly is a magical moment, but it doesn't happen without a courtship and ultimately the choice of the bride. The groom may choose his bride many months or years before she is ready. He woos, courts, loves, prepares, asks, and … waits. Oh, he desperately desires to hear those three little letters wrapped together, one tiny little word that can bring the promise of life and joy. With just a "yes," he hears "I love you. I trust you. I want to spend my life with you. I want to be yours and for you to be mine forever."

Through sickness and health, good times and bad, 'til death do you part … until you meet again.

God is in love with us and desires for us to choose to love him. For him to know you love him, *your love must be a choice.* Love cannot be coerced. To sincerely and with a clear head choose love (not just an infatuation), one must count the cost and act on free will. There is ALWAYS an alternative to love. There is always a choice when facing this vulnerability.

My personal definition of a healthy relationship is an *ever-increasing knowledge of each other.* Think of any relationship where one or both of the parties stopped learning about the other. You know that couple, the older couple at Denny's, sitting there for an hour through ordering, eating dinner, dessert, coffee, without ever exchanging a word, never giving a knowing glance, smile, or even a frown. They've run out of words. They have come to the place of believing there's nothing left to know of their partner. Funny, I bet they're sitting there wondering what the other person is thinking.

If we were created to be in relationship with God, and if a healthy relationship is an ever-increasing knowledge of each other, then *our purpose in living is to know God more every day.* Doing so reveals a true perspective of ourselves and others that leads us back to grace.

When we actively pursue knowing the One who loves us the most, we see him in all his glory and see ourselves in that reflection. We see ourselves as a beautiful bride: adored, cared for, sacrificed for—but desiring the strength, structure, and love of another. Yes, God knows everything about our past and everything about our future, and he still sees us as his beautiful bride. He won't wake up in a year and wonder how he got here and if it was all a big mistake.

BOTTOM LINE

Get to know this God, this Lover, because the closer you get, the more you recognize your need and appreciate the fact that he chose you. It's a beautiful thing to be loved by someone you don't deserve. Realizing that is truth and responding accordingly is a sign of a very healthy relationship.

 TALK TO GOD:

Ask for God's Spirit to guide your thoughts and prayers, and then be quiet for a little while. Speak freely, as if you were speaking to your spouse, but focus everything you say on loving words of appreciation. Tell Jesus what you love about him and why you chose to spend your life with him for all eternity.

 DIG DEEPER:

Think of Jesus as someone you would consider marrying (guys, make a serious effort). Make a list of the things about him that create a desire in you for a lifelong relationship. What else would be required for you to take the plunge into marriage? Now, accepting that you already are married to Jesus, think about how you can grow in your relationship by accepting what's missing and doing what is in your power to grow in knowledge of your spouse.

Question 11

"What Does God Expect of Me?"

"You did not choose me, but I chose you and appointed you to go and bear fruit—fruit that will last. Then the Father will give you whatever you ask in my name. This is my command: Love each other."

John 15:16–17

"Uh-oh, God gave me this great gift of forgiveness, so there must be a catch, right?"

Are you waiting for the other shoe to drop? Sure, you heard that the gift of grace was free, but that was then. Now you are signed up to this "Christian life" and you think there must be responsibilities as you live it out. Okay, there are, but not for the reason you might expect.

God doesn't expect all Christians to build monuments to him, give all of our money, abandon our jobs and become foreign missionaries, live a life of poverty, or take a vow of lifelong chastity. He leads some people down those paths, but not most of us. Not by a long shot.

Nope, God's desire for you—what he really, really wants—is just more of why you turned to him in the first place. He wants you to fully understand your need for him so that you can know the depths of his love for you. And when you come to realize something of that love, you can't help but share in his passion to love others and be in relationship with them like he is with you. He wants you to be involved in their relationship with him, just like other believers were involved in you discovering Jesus for yourself.

One of the ways God helps us do that is by simply learning to love other people. Why? Because most people aren't very lovable. You probably think the same about yourself on occasion, or maybe often. Love, *real* love, requires nothing in return: no expectation of "proper" response, no love returned, not even good feelings for you. That kind of love is beyond us. Frankly, it's impossible without God.

God calls us to love others for the same reason he encourages us to do anything—so we can know him more.

Can you genuinely desire good things for your enemies?

Are you just dying to give gifts to the person who stole from you?

Do you have compassion for that really rude, selfish person at work?

What about that Hummer-driving, two-lane-hogging, oblivious-to-the-world maniac who just passed you on the highway with the cell phone surgically attached to his ear?

Take note: I'm not just talking about loving non-Christians. Oh no, you can expect such behavior from people who don't know God, and it is often easier to forgive. It's the churchgoers that you may find most difficult to love when they fail. People will always disappoint, and God knew that.

BOTTOM LINE

For you to continually seek God, you must regularly find yourself in need of more than you can muster. You may have plenty of money, time, joy, and good things in your life, but you will never be able to love unconditionally without leaning on God. If you seek to love just one person whom you wouldn't normally include in your circle of friends, your picture of who God is and what he is capable of will radically change. God wants to make you uncomfortable so you run to him for comfort. Ask God for this gift, and he will surely answer.

 TALK TO GOD:

Have a conversation with God today about getting help in learning to understand love. Ask him for an opportunity to love someone you normally wouldn't, and then keep your eyes and ears open.

DIG DEEPER:

Look up verses on love starting with any of the Gospel books (Matthew, Mark, Luke, and John), searching for any time Jesus uses the word. Some Bibles print words spoken by Jesus in red to make them easier to locate. Ask for guidance from the Holy Spirit to help you understand God's perspective on what true love really is. Take one short verse that particularly strikes a chord and write it down to memorize. Carry it in your car, at work, etc., and try to recite it from memory, along with the address (chapter and verse numbers), whenever you have a spare moment. You will notice very soon that the Holy Spirit will bring memorized verses to mind at critical times. It's like feeding ammunition to a soldier in battle.

Question 12

"What Should I Expect of God?"

The fear of the LORD is the beginning of wisdom.

Psalm 111:10

The Bible tells us that Christian living is about freedom, and we often try to define that freedom as change in life circumstances—a purely subjective and ever-changing definition. Think for yourself about some circumstances you desperately desired to change at one time, only to find later that what you desired was the worst thing that could have happened. Have you ever desired the love of the wrong person, hoped for the wrong job, or dreamed of the wrong toy? Oh, how deflating and empty the realization of a wrong desire fulfilled!

Life is rife with unmet expectations. The limited wisdom

of man and the inability to see beyond our circumstance and time guarantee that any hope for specific situational results and outcomes will often be wrong. If you pull the dresser of expectations out from the wall and peer behind, you will find hidden in the corner what you truly believe about God. Our disappointments with life, people, or ourselves are all rooted in what we believe about God.

Expectations of God, right or wrong, are the root of everything good or bad, frustrating or joyous, in the Christian.

A.W. Tozer says, *"What comes into our minds when we think about God is the most important thing about us. ... the most portentous fact about any man is not what he at a given time may say or do, but what he in his deep heart conceives God to be like. We tend by a secret law of the soul to move toward our mental image of God.*

Were we able to extract from any man a complete answer to the question, 'What comes into your mind when you think about God?' we might predict with certainty the spiritual future of that man.[3]

How we see God defines how we see ourselves, our circumstances, our lives, our futures, the church, and others. Through the filter of our perception of God in the eye of our heart are determined our actions and emotions.

Once you have answered the question "*Is he?*" with a "yes," you are led to "What is he like?" which invariably leads to "What must I do about him?"[4]

The foundation of every good decision lies within these few questions. God knows himself perfectly and longs to be perfectly known by us. God understands that for us to know his love and to love him in return, we must know him because he is love. He is also good and holy and eternal—and so many more things that will enrich our Christian life as we understand them by knowing him. He wants knowing him to be our greatest priority. He made everything in the heavens and earth as object lessons for a deeper understanding of him.

God also expects us to maintain a healthy fear of him. *"So, as we learn more about God we become more and more afraid?"* Not very appealing, huh? Thankfully, that's not an accurate depiction of biblical truth. To fear God means to know his power and holiness and see your comparative weakness and need. It does not mean you shrink away and huddle in a corner—quite the opposite, actually.

Think about fire. Fire has enabled man to achieve far beyond his early dreams. It helps us stay warm when it's cold, cook and preserve foods, and create materials for buildings and clothes. Fire can be both productive and destructive. It can bring life or death. There are aspects of fire that are too terrifying and mysterious to understand. There are aspects of fire that we can study and use to our advantage. We have learned to harness the impact of fire and predict its behavior in certain situations. But any firefighter will tell you that a wise person maintains a healthy fear of fire at all times.

God is often compared to an all-consuming fire.

He deserves to be approached with respect—not because he intends to harm us. On the contrary, he wants us to understand what he has made available to us—the heights and depths of his power. The fear of God is the beginning of wisdom, because when we see God as all-powerful, all-loving, and desiring to manifest himself fully in us, we trust in his Spirit to guide us and teach us in all things. So, as we go about life doing as God leads, trusting in that guidance and purpose, we make right choices and are found to be wise.

Regardless of how long it takes you to travel this road or how many times you trudge down that path, there is always the promise of the knowledge and fear of God as your destination.

As you travel this road you will discover deeper truths of God than you ever imagined. What was in your head will move deep into your soul. Intellectual knowledge will become true "knowing" in a way that requires no further questioning. Your picture of God will become that rock that doesn't move—the foundation where all of what you do and become is built. You will even be okay with the unanswerable questions, because knowing would change nothing of the truth that is rock-solid certain.

BOTTOM LINE

Expect God to love you, but not to make you comfortable. Expect God to reveal truth, but only what truth you can handle at the time. Expect God to challenge you, but to remain patient with your failures. Expect God to relentlessly pursue change in you, but don't expect to guess his methods or timing. And above all, expect God to be good. He will be nothing but.

TALK TO GOD:

Today, thank God for his incredible wisdom. Praise him for prayers left unanswered. If that is difficult, ask God to help you with areas in which you might still need to develop trust, then thank him again for his patience and kindness. Ask God to help you develop an understanding of his power and an appreciation that his greatness is more than you will ever grasp or understand.

 DIG DEEPER:

Think about something powerful, like fire, but that is also very useful and helpful. When do you not fear it? When is it dangerous? How can respect for the power of fire relate to understanding God?

Question 13

"How Do I Pray?"

The Spirit helps us in our weakness. We do not know what we ought to pray for, but the Spirit himself intercedes for us with groans that words cannot express.

Romans 8:26

It began with a prayer and it will likely end with one—your life on earth in relationship with God. It is in prayer that we hear his voice in the midst of our words, identify his intention and message through his Word (reading and meditating on the Bible), and can finally make sense of our circumstances.

The very act of prayer is a step of faith. If you don't believe God is listening, that he cares to speak to you, and that there is some purpose in speaking to him, then you are surely wasting your time. Perhaps you started praying as part of the pre-intimate time of asking him to become a reality to you. That's what happened on my route from atheism. After I came to the conclusion that God must exist, I was faced with a dilemma. All of the scientific theory I trusted was incomplete and contradictory (such as the Big Bang contradicting basic laws of science without a "Banger"). It struck me that if there truly was a being powerful enough to create the universe, and for some reason that entity chose to create me, I had better figure out why.

So, I resolved to strike up a conversation with God, but I didn't really know how. Just at that time, the church I attended held a small class entitled "How to Pray." I arrived on the first day armed with many questions, but hoping for anonymity. I found the anonymity part impossible since only myself, another woman who already believed in Jesus, and the two leaders were in attendance. All of a sudden, my questions became the center of our weekly discussions:

> Do you have to kneel and hold your hands a certain way? Can you pray during the day? Do you need to say anything in particular? Will I offend God if I say the wrong thing? How do I ask questions in a way that I can get answers? Everyone seems to pray with such pretty words, words I sometimes don't even understand, but I can't do that. Where do I start?

We looked at many scriptures that gave more context to my ideas about prayer, yet one truth really struck me, leaving its mark on me to this day. It is wrapped up in two words: *honesty* and *trust*. In the Psalms, King David would rant and rave, cry out and plead. He was honest with his emotions. He never pretended. He didn't worry that his way of praying might offend God or inhibit God's response. He understood that God could hear beyond his words into his deepest heart. The night before he went to the cross, Jesus experienced similar prayer. Here was the one who had the most intimate relationship with God. Yet he was so distraught during his prayers that final night that he sweat blood, exhibiting a rare condition that has been occasionally recorded in history, occurring only under the most immense emotional stress. Jesus, who was well practiced in prayer, poured out his doubts without reservation and then yielded to his Father's will. Honest communication—however joyous or painful—with trust that God is wiser, all loving, and in control is the pattern of prayer expressed by godly men and women in the Bible.

> Why, if God is all-powerful, all-knowing, and will always have his will done, do we even need to pray? Doesn't he know what we're going to say anyway? What's the point?

What you're really asking is "What's my purpose?" We were made to know God and glorify him—forever. It's the very reason mankind was created. We don't pray because God needs it—we pray because *we* need it. There's something remarkable that happens to us in prayer. In those moments in conversation with God, *we* change.

Athletes know about rest. The great irony is that exercise actually destroys muscles; it physically breaks them down. Strength comes during sleep. When an athlete sleeps, what's damaged can finally be healed and become greater than before. Red blood cells—the oxygen-carrying source of life—are also used during exercise and manufactured during sleep. Healthy and abundant red blood cells are so key to endurance that many world-class athletes sleep in plastic tents (designed to simulate the low oxygen found at high altitudes) to stress the body into producing an excess. So both our strength and our endurance are born, not of work only, but of rest from work.

If you go about your life doing and doing and doing, without connecting to God, you'll eventually collapse just like an athlete who never finds rest. We were created for the balance of trials and healing. And our *healing*—our ability to go about our *doing* with proper perspective, motivation, and strength—comes from *reconnecting* to our source, from finding our center. That center is our purpose for existence. That center is found in the reality of God, in the increasing knowledge of his love and power.

What enables an athlete to grow, heal, and improve is the acceptance that rest is critical. What enables you to grow, heal, and improve is the faith that prayer is even more critical. Beyond the obvious, there is something that happens when we fulfill our purpose in existence, when we ride with the current of God's intention. Living can become peaceful even when life is chaotic. When you face God and seek to color in his face a little, to peer a little behind the curtain and get a better understanding of what he is truly like, you finally see yourself and your circumstances clearly—and God is glorified. We must pray or that purpose is never found—we never heal and God is never glorified.

What do you know about God? What do you feel about God? What do you not understand and want to know about God? What do you doubt? What makes you sad? What does that say about your idea of what God is like? What makes you happy? What does that say about your idea of God? How have you recognized God's work in your life? What does the Bible say about his role? What do you believe? What do you want to believe? What is God trying to teach you or change in you because of the circumstances that now concern you?

This isn't about what to say in prayer or how to say it, it is about why you say anything at all and why you listen intently for answers and words of truth. God desires to take the responsibility of our burdens and keep us from worry, and he will even take the responsibility of how we pray. It is the voice of God that guides our prayers if we allow God that freedom, but too often prayer is focused on just our desires and not seeking God's—too much telling and very little listening. In prayer you can seek grace or gifts, sobriety or Santa Claus, and freedom or fault; but ultimately prayer is about seeking a greater understanding of God. Sounds like a very important thing for you, doesn't it? It is, but it isn't as difficult as we often try to make it.

Jesus told us to make our prayers honest and genuine. Sometimes prayer is to be a personal thing between you and God, and at other times it is to be with others in order to build each other up. Always it is to be focused on God, without concern for how others see you, or desire to receive anything other than truth from him. Christ said you should come to God as a little child—full of trust and need and a sense of his loving authority in our lives. He never said you should speak a certain way or say specific words, but he did give examples and guidance.

Most important, though, is *why* you pray, not so much *how*. That is the indication of the condition of your heart, which is what God is always most concerned about in your life. When you don't know what to pray, just begin. Speak truth. And take time to listen between your words. It is the spaces between notes—the rests—that make music beautiful.

BOTTOM LINE

Pray alone; pray together; pray to avoid temptation; pray for those who persecute you; pray for today's needs; pray for forgiveness for others and yourself; pray and make your requests known to God. But in all prayers acknowledge God's power and holiness, and all will eventually be well in your soul. When God becomes as big to you as he desires you to know, no circumstance, whether past, present, or perceived in the future, can possibly cast a shadow upon that wonderful truth. And in the shadow of that big God you can find rest.

 TALK TO GOD:

Is there something you have held back from saying to God? Tell him now. He already knows, but there's something that happens in your soul when you trust him with your words and actions. Any confusion, any frustration, any confession, any fear—say it. Then tell God something good that you know is true about him.

Dig Deeper:

If we don't ask of our Father, who gets the credit for the good? If we don't communicate our feelings and desires, at what point can they be influenced and aligned with God's desires for us? If we don't take time to speak truth about God, when do we begin to believe it? When are we reminded of what we so easily forget? How can we change, become greater than ourselves, if we solely rely on ourselves? Read Luke 18:10–14. Look for other verses where Christ spoke about prayer and look for common themes.

Question 14

"Will God Let Me Fail?"

"I am the LORD your God, who teaches you what is best for you, who directs you in the way you should go. If only you had paid attention to my commands, your peace would have been like a river, your righteousness like the waves of the sea."

Isaiah 48:17–18

God's sauna—Phoenix, Arizona in July. An air temperature of 105 degrees Fahrenheit caused the hot asphalt to melt my tennis shoes. I read an article in the local newspaper about a woman who, overcome by the heat, passed out waiting for a bus and fell onto the street. Only seconds later, she was lifted to the sidewalk, but not before receiving third degree burns to her face. "But it's a dryyyyyyy heat." Yeah, and the atomic bomb that leveled Hiroshima was a "controlled explosion."

Maggie, my dog, and I were out for an ill-advised walk in the middle of the day. Her excessive energy and my lack of it were making for a rather non-productive afternoon for this writer. We both needed a break outside. Even with a hope that the sun would rejuvenate my mind and sap her body, I had no idea the extreme to which that wish would occur.

Although I lived in the city, there was a large empty lot at the end of the cul-de-sac where Maggie would often take me to play ball, chase the occasional cat, and flush the odd dove. Bounding after the first toss of the ball that afternoon, she suddenly stopped cold in her tracks, ears at attention, right paw ever so gently rising from the ground. Pounce! Five or six feathery rockets erupted from silos hidden in the tall grass. Maggie barked with typical authority and glee, but what's this? One of the scuds stayed low and Maggie joined in hot pursuit.

Flying down the street, they serpentined back and forth, so fast and far I quickly lost sight. I was praying, yelling, and running as the three of us headed straight for a busy five lane road, bird fleeing for its life, Maggie so focused on her desire she was oblivious to my instruction. Feeling quickly exhausted in the stifling heat, my heart leapt when I saw her finally move toward me, and then screeched to a halt when I realized she could hardly walk.

Even though she stopped before running to her death in the busy street, her disobedience had left its mark. The heat of the pavement ripped every pad off all four feet and now that the object of her desire was gone, she realized her pain. Maggie is normally totally obedient (I once stopped her mid pounce on a rabbit with a simple "NO"), but this time she was so focused she didn't hear me. Sure, I could have kept her on the leash, and some would say I always should, but in my mind her past obedience gave her certain freedoms. Her choice to not listen and obey this time robbed me of the opportunity to protect her. She walked with little protective "footies" and a pronounced limp for many days and went a bit nuts not being able to play ball for two weeks, but she soon healed and life got back to normal—with the exception that she listened even more carefully than before.

Yes, Maggie lost some energy that day, but we both gained much more. Although I didn't get back to my writing that afternoon, I was inspired by how much I was like my dog. God gives us all free will. We operate off leash, so we can up and run off if we choose. However, we are expected to follow voice commands—the voice of our Master—if we are to stay safe and get the most out of life. Temporary enticements can distract us from the safety of God. The good news is that he will ceaselessly call after us and, when we turn, he will bind up our wounds, give us rest, and help us to health and greater wisdom. The beautiful thing is that even after our disobedience he invites us on another walk—off leash again.

BOTTOM LINE

God does not desire you to experience pain or failure, but he can use your bad choices, and the bad choices of others leading to the hurtful state of the world, to accomplish what he truly desires. God wants you to know him as your Lord and your God. That means he wants you to know peace and joy in the confidence of his power and love despite what the world throws at you. When you ignore his instruction, you will ultimately fail in fulfilling your purpose and it will hurt. He will call after you and he might make your path more difficult so that you will turn around, but he won't force you to love him. God wants your obedience to come from love and recognition of who he is. You are walking off leash. Choose to heel to the voice of the Master and you will walk in freedom and joy. Choose disobedience and you'll get burned.

TALK TO GOD:

Ask God to search your heart to see if there is any disobedience in you—something that you are unwilling to let go of and can't yet trust to God. Is there some area of your life you can't let go of because you're not sure you believe his promise to provide a greater pleasure? Confess what he reveals and ask forgiveness if that is what you truly want. Ask for help in turning from sin and for a growing desire to learn greater obedience.

DIG DEEPER:

Take an objective look at your life, at least as much as you can. Is there anything you would not be willing to give up if God asked you to? Read Luke 14:25–33, but don't be discouraged. God wants you to grow to love him so much that you would be willing to abandon all for his sake. He may never ask that, but he knows you will find great freedom when your heart is that committed. Imagine how you could live differently if you were completely committed to God's desires for you and completely trusting that God is good.

Question 15

"I Messed Up, What Do I Do Now?"

Therefore, there is now no condemnation for those who are in Christ Jesus, because through Christ Jesus the law of the Spirit of life set me free from the law of sin and death.

Romans 8:1–2

After accepting Christ, you become a new creation. You may experience a few days or even months of emotional bliss before the old you does the thing you swore you would never do again. Whether it's sleeping with someone, feeding an addiction, or just stretching the truth, it catches you by surprise. When it happens, you are disappointed with yourself and often believe God feels the same.

When it happened to me, I questioned everything—my salvation, whether God would ever listen again, and whether I could tell anyone. I considered just packing it in and returning to the old life. But that wasn't an option. The old life was dead, and turning away from Christ wouldn't change my heart back. So, after awhile I turned back to God, confessed my sin, and began the sobering, yet beautiful, lifelong pattern of turning bit after bit of my life over to God. Each time new areas of weakness in my character or pain from my past was revealed, I relinquished them to God. In time, the process became easier, and to my surprise, it actually began to feel normal and full of hope.

If you expected you would be free from your old patterns and influences, you are very likely wrong. All of those things that gave you temporary pleasure or a sense of safety, but left you feeling empty and dirty inside, are all still there lurking about, wooing you back, lying to you that you belong with them. Don't listen.

You see, the guilt you feel isn't coming from that thing you did wrong, it's from God. The fact that you feel bad is proof that God loves you. God wants to free you from any lie telling you that you are in need of something other than him to feel whole; his Spirit is there to point out what you must let go.

Today you messed up and God told you he knows. But at the same time, he's saying, "I love you. I'll forgive what you did. More importantly, I want you to be free from whatever led you to do it. I want you to become the person you were created to be, and I'll help you get there if you trust me."

God doesn't heal sin, he forgives it. God heals what is inside your head that leads you to sin. Don't run from God and hide—ever. It's rather pointless and silly anyway, since he already knows everything. He shows you your sin so that you can stand side by side and look at it together, arm in arm, and start working on it. The bad things you do, the things that make you feel like a failure, or the things that make you feel dirty are not barriers between you and God anymore. They are simply the next things on the list for you and God to deal with as you move on to greater peace and freedom.

BOTTOM LINE

Embrace this moment. Admit to God what you did. Ask for his forgiveness and help to no longer conform to those patterns. Confess to someone you trust and move on with life. You are no longer condemned for what you do. There is a big difference between conviction and condemnation. The former will happen regularly until you die, but the latter only sticks around by your choice. Trust me, it is no friend. Let it go.

 TALK TO GOD:

Think about something from your past or your present that you maybe haven't trusted to anyone—a secret you are afraid someone will learn. Choose to trust God with it. Ask for forgiveness. Talk to him about why you hesitate in trusting him.

 DIG DEEPER:

Read 1 Corinthians 10:13. List the promises God makes to you in this verse. Will you choose to accept grace and receive God's power or let it overcome you? It is simply a choice.

Question 16

"Do I Need Help?"

Is any one of you in trouble? He should pray. Is anyone happy?
Let him sing songs of praise. Is any one of you sick? He should
call the elders of the church to pray over him and anoint him with
oil in the name of the Lord. And the prayer offered in faith will
make the sick person well; the Lord will raise him up. If he has
sinned, he will be forgiven. Therefore confess your sins to each
other and pray for each other so that you may be healed.

James 5:13–16

There we were: me, and this dearly loved person with her suit-case full of one week's clothing, toiletries, ID, Bible, and $150 that I gave her for spending money—the list of allowable items for a month-long stay.

First day of rehab.

As I sat with Kara today in the admissions office filling out a mountain of paperwork, the director searched her bags as gently and kindly as he could, making small talk to keep her from feeling like a criminal as he peered into every pocket and crevice for contraband. The half-full bottle of multi-vitamins had to go ... already opened. I guess some people have gone so far as to taint vitamins with drugs, but that's not her problem. Nope, in addition to suffering from depression and an addiction to nicotine, she's an alcoholic.

This intelligent, vibrant, talented, and yes, Christian, forty-year-old woman was entering "rehab." In the few days leading to this moment, she was ashamed, sad, in denial, and sometimes quite angry; but that day, she was mostly just humbled and resolute. It took a while to get here, but she eventually arrived on the train of God's perfect timing.

About seventeen months earlier Kara had accepted Christ. Contemplating suicide with a fistful of pills, she hit rock bottom after life threw her too many curves to swing at. She found God when she finally found herself powerless. You may have heard this story many times. Sometimes discovering the depths of hell on earth is required in order to give up control of your life, admit your need, and trust in God. You think, *She's saved now, so this should be a wonderfully tragic story with a happy ending*, right? Well, after death that's guaranteed, but what about the days between now and then? How does she live today with the impact of her life before Christ?

Kara just reached Phase 2 in the life of the adult convert. There was no doubt she was saved. This we both knew because the gentle and persistent hand of the Holy Spirit had begun to lovingly peel her onion, one smelly layer at a time. For months, she had been getting her life in order, reconnecting with family and moving halfway across the country to start anew. Only after a year pursuing God and reattaching to relationships with people who cared for her was she finally ready to take an honest look at the state she was in. Only then was she able to recognize the soreness—bruises and scars left from a lifetime fighting for survival in a pit of despair.

Some people realize their need for help from others on the day they turn to God. For others it takes much longer. No matter how old you are when you embrace God, life has left its mark on you. God can heal you, but you must recognize what needs healing and where you need to go to receive the best treatment.

My friend Kara realized it took more than a good counselor or spiritual guide to take the next step of freedom. Everything she thought about herself and what life should look like needed re-examination. But no matter what your situation, just like Kara, your needs will become known a little at a time and always with the help of another's perspective. That's why becoming spiritually mature requires you to engage in relationship with other people who also trust Christ, so you can find people whose opinions are objective and worthy of trust.

Do you get the sense that God is tapping you on the shoulder and asking you to look at a specific aspect of your life? Are there patterns to the concerns voiced by friends or family? Are you pursuing those answers or trying to deny their reality? Is there something you think you should do but aren't doing?

When you accept Christ, your eternity may be addressed, as well as your immediate desperation. However, your remaining time on this planet is fraught with choices—choices that you will often fail at no matter how hard you try, especially early on.

The choices you make after accepting Christ are dictated by a perpetual conflict of "Life-Lies" vs. "Spiritual Truth." Life-Lies are the etched patterns of emotional response to life lived without God's Spirit and initially feel truer than anything because they're what you've always known; but truth is found only in God's true character. Unfortunately, what you know about God determines what you accept about yourself, and ignorance often reigns supreme as a new Christian.

You need "Truth-Speakers" in your life. You need people who are mature enough in their own faith to distinguish between "Life-Lies" and "Spiritual Truths." God will sometimes use nonbelievers to speak truth into your life as well. We all need help from time to time—the question is whether or not you will be open to it when the time comes.

BOTTOM LINE

It's time to step out and start trusting God through trusting other people. You can't do this alone. Life was not made to be lived outside of relationship because you were made to be known.

 TALK TO GOD:

Thank God for the faith you do have, but also ask him to help you with your areas of unbelief. Thank Jesus for dying and rising again so that all believers could carry his Spirit to guide and teach them in all things. Have a conversation with Jesus about what he thinks of the church.

Dig Deeper:

Spend some time thinking about people in your life you fully trusted. If there was someone to whom you could tell any secret and share your fears, hopes, and dreams with, what enabled them to gain that place in your life? Think of what you could do that would enable you to grow in trust of God.

Question 17

"Why Read the Bible?"

Jesus answered, "It is written: 'Man does not live on bread alone, but on every word that comes from the mouth of God.'"

Matthew 4:4

Two thousand four hundred thirty-two whisper-thin pages with gold-leafed edges, maps and references, dictionary and word charts, name embossed on the front, and that built-in little ribbon bookmark ... it is called the Bible. This five-pound monstrosity of a book sitting on the table before me may have rivals in physical stature among the great classics of literature, such as Tolstoy's *War and Peace* or Homer's *Iliad*, but nothing, nada, zero, has ever surpassed it in impact.

At first glance, this book with its unique design, this

Bible, appears as compelling as a phone book—without even enough pictures to maintain your interest or enough structure to make your searching fruitful. It isn't written chronologically so as to be easily read from cover to cover. It doesn't even appear to be a story, but rather a collection of stories, some even repeated numerous times, written by between forty and fifty scribes—most known, a handful assumed.

Why on earth is it so important?

Over thousands of years, this book in its many pieces and forms was copied and distributed and read and translated and copied over and over and over. Even to this day, dedicated teams travel the world, learning ancient tongues spoken only in remote areas of faraway jungles, in order to translate this text into native, tribal languages of indigenous people. There are numerous interpretations in the vernacular of many ages, from the original Aramaic and Hebrew texts written on sheepskins, stones, and primitive paper; to the King James version penned many centuries ago in Olde English with its arduous *thee*s and *thou*s; to the more recent *The Message* peppered with modern colloquialisms and word pictures. Yes, it has been translated many times into many tongues. But within the message of this text, more so than the method of translation, many people dispute details and search for seeming contradictions—although no one can dispute the massive and unique impact of these words.

The greatest art, music, poetry, and literature were inspired by the message of these words. From the likes of Rembrandt, Michelangelo, Beethoven, Handel, Bach, Dante, Milton, Tolstoy, and countless others come many facets of expression of the same message. The combined literature of the greatest thinkers and philosophers of all time, from Plato to Socrates and Aristotle, has paled in comparison to its impact. No other work has inspired so many great thinkers and artists, but it was written by simple men, many admittedly inarticulate.

No book has been read over and over in part or whole by more people, in more languages, in more years—nor had more books written about it—than the Bible. What is it about this book? Much of it contains mundane and boring lists of families and details about times gone past. Frankly, none of these words seem incredibly inspiring when looked at as simply another piece of literature. No, there is something more unique about this book than its gold leaf and its consistent topping of the best-seller lists in all its many forms.

Why is it so important? Is there something in the book itself? Or in the words? Or is it something else—like some magical spell it casts upon the reader?

Yes and no. As a child, I thought the book itself had some special properties and so I treated it gingerly. I was quite confused when I saw my grandparents writing in it, underlining, taking notes in the margins—something I wasn't even allowed to do with my own little picture books. They obviously loved this book since they read it so often, yet they seemed to treat it with a combination of a sense of treasure and contempt. That was only the first of a long line of confusing contradictions that persisted in me for decades with this book.

I have observed people as they study this book. I've watched some of them come face to face with nothing but words, walking away frustrated and angry. Others have come face to face with their souls and experienced radical change in their very being from a simple line on a randomly opened page. Each may have started as a skeptic, both read the same book, yet both experienced something different.

A young Russian from a very small town tells the story of her rebellious mother during communist times. For seventy years, the Bible was at the top of a list of banned books, and if you were caught with one, you could be jailed or sent away, never to be heard from again. This woman, although she had no faith in God, was not fond of the restrictions and secretly kept a Bible as her private way of saying "I will not be controlled!" Owning the Bible did not change the woman, but her daughter read that book whenever she felt oppressed and found freedom from the impact of her circumstances. Years later, because of this book, not only did she become a radically different person, but she began to help others discover the truth she found. Instead of hatred and rebellion growing and burning in her heart, she became compassionate, caring, and lived a life of serving others. She found peace through simple letters arranged in groups, separated by symbols and spaces.

Or did she?

I know a man, a friend of mine, who grew up in the heart of the American Bible Belt: Atlanta, Georgia. He went to church, and read and studied the Bible his entire life, with no impact whatsoever to his character or sense of peace. He strived in business and found success in the form of power and money. As he entered his forties with the attainment of every major life goal set in the previous two decades, his definition of success changed. Suddenly none of it mattered and he was in despair. With a fistful of dollars and a garage full of fast cars that claim to be able to catch anything in a flash, peace remained ever elusive.

Out of desperation, he turned to those letters, symbols, and spaces in search of solace, in search of truth. This time he found what he was looking for, and he was forever changed. He learned of God's desire to have us know him and how our selfish rebellion kept us apart. He read of Jesus' sacrifice so that we could be reunited with God, and he believed.

A week later he said, "The strangest thing has happened to me. I can't stop reading the Bible."

"Why?" I asked.

"Oh, that's simple, now I know the author."

This book is not merely letters, numbers, spaces, and symbols—nor is it opinions, conjecture, or fables. The words in this book can change lives, but only if those lives are in pursuit of change and are looking for truth within the words.

For these words to have the impact that is so often acclaimed, there must be something beyond the mere text at work here.

The answer is found in the combination of the author, the message, the interpreter, and the heart of the reader.

The Bible is a story told in many parts, from many perspectives, but always with a constant theme and purpose. This is the story of God and his desire for relationship with man. The ups and downs of that relationship—the rejection and forgiveness, the personalities and disputes, the pursuit and denial—are all the same story. Although the characters change, the hero of the story doesn't. God has remained consistent throughout, but it took an entire book, thousands of pages, and many perspectives to describe him.

This book tells of his purity and holiness, his requirement

for truth and justice, and our failure to accomplish any of that for ourselves. It tells of his love, repeated forgiveness and grace, and his desperate pursuit of our love. It tells of the incredible patience of God and selfishness of man. It tells of the path of reconciliation provided for that relationship, and how to live once reunited. This book is the ultimate love story, peppered with high adventure and historical fact, and you are one of the main characters.

The Bible tells all those things, but without the inspiration of the Spirit of God, it merely leads you to the decision to believe or not to believe, and does little to change you. If a person chooses not to believe this story, nothing will happen to him. But you—the one who chose to believe—you can change with every page turned.

He says that if you seek truth you will find it. You have chosen to believe in God and Christ's sacrifice; therefore, you have been given a gift. You have been given the great interpreter of God's voice called Holy Spirit. The Bible, now with the interpretation the Spirit provides, is like the subtitles to a foreign film. You can understand very little of the movie without them and sit for hours merely guessing and getting frustrated, or you can read the subtitles and interpret what's going on.

Once you learn the characters, the plot, the themes, and the message of the movie through the leading of the interpretation, you can begin to even think past the immediate action and dialogue into what might happen. While watching a good film, you become a participant in the emotion and action, rising above your red fabric seat and sticky shoes, and are transported into another place and time. You experience something other than words and pictures, just like when you read the Bible with proper interpretation. When you listen for God's voice within the pages of the Bible—his Word—and ask for the interpretation from the Spirit of God, his voice begins to become clear and you are injected into the pages. The story becomes about you and God, and you are changed because it is found to be truth and not fantasy. Instead of experiencing temporary escape from reality, you are transported into reality.

It's a difficult thing to grasp at first, but if you think of these words as the truth of God that he desires to communicate to us, straight from his mouth into the hands of scribes, these words are empowered to become more than literature.

God inspired man to write down these truths because he wants to be known, and as we have discussed, only when we begin to see God clearly can we see ourselves with right eyes. Anyone seeking truth above comfort will meet God within its pages and, after some growing pains, will eventually wallow in the comfort of their creator. And that is precisely why so many do not see anything but words. They have neither the desire for truth nor the interpreter of the message; therefore the message has no impact.

I know this sounds a bit confusing, but if you believe that God desperately wants us to be in intimate relationship with him, then don't you think he would want to communicate to us? Don't you think that he would make it so we could have conversations? He calls himself the Great Counselor, Father, our lover, and our groom. That's pretty intimate, but he means it.

There is freedom in this book and it should be your lifetime pursuit to find God's voice within its pages. What are you doing about it today? Are you asking for help? Are you skimming or searching for truth? Are you seeking confirmation for what you want it to say or seeking what God wants to tell you?

There is another truth at play here. Nothing I have said about the Bible will really make much sense until you experience it yourself. When you read something you've read many times and it suddenly jumps off the page, grabs your heart, and drops you to your knees, you will realize God is alive, his Spirit is within you, and your life is like a vine seeking its very nourishment from this source. You will see that what once felt more like science fiction is now a historical fact from personal experience. And then you will want to tell others.

BOTTOM LINE

If you read and learn to properly interpret the Bible, guided by the Holy Spirit, you will change. If you try to live your Christian life apart from God's Word, his voice will remain distant. It's the way he made it. It's just the way it is.

God is alive and he's speaking—read the subtitles.

TALK TO GOD:

Ask God's Spirit to guide your prayers, then spend a few minutes silently thinking about the amazing fact that God—the all-powerful Creator of the universe—wants to talk to you in very intimate ways, with very personal words. Tell him what you think about that privilege and the gift of the Bible.

 ## DIG DEEPER:

Read Psalm 18 and for every verse write down a symbolic parallel to your own life (e.g., What can God do to protect you from your enemies?) or acknowledge what he has already done in that area.

Question 18

"What Is Success?"

And without faith it is impossible to please God.

Hebrews 11:6

What does he want from me?" Jim said as his head hung low, eyes focused on the ground just a millimeter above his self-esteem. "I volunteer at church, try to do the right things, but still I feel he is disappointed. I feel like nothing I do will please God."

"Yeah, Jim, you're right. You can't please God by anything you do."

That wasn't the response my friend expected, but it was precisely the reality he needed to grasp. The fact that he didn't understand it, after years and years of following Christ, revealed that the most basic but most important truth of the

Christian life yet eluded him. As a result, true joy was destined to remain just as elusive. To avoid Jim's joy-sapping path, there is something you must seek to understand now, although it will continue to amaze and astound you throughout your life: you can't please God by anything you *do*.

The reality of this truth reveals the essence of what God expects of you, what he desires you to know about him, and what he will continue to teach you until the day you die. To be more specific, the things you do—not because you do them, but rather *why* you do them and *what* happens in you because you do them is what's important. You see, God is only concerned about the condition of your heart and the product of his efforts through you, so he gets the credit when you admit there is not anything you can do completely on your own.

Remember back to when we were discussing your purpose in living—to know God more every day? To help you fulfill that purpose, God will certainly do his part, which means he will constantly put you into situations that deepen your understanding of his character and love. To grasp the truth of his power, you must find yourself powerless. To understand his grace, you must fail. Only through this path will God be glorified by your actions.

This runs completely counter to the idea that God desires us to be happy and comfortable all the time. When God receives more credit than you, it is likely that you are doing something that is beyond your ability (emotionally, physically, relationally, or otherwise) and are forced to trust him in the process. This means that you were most definitely made uncomfortable, taken out of a known place, and stretched a bit.

God does not expect you to be successful all the time. God does not expect that you will get it right (whatever *it* is). God does not expect perfection or an undying desire to *try* hard all the time.

God expects you to trust him. That's it. He expects you to rely on him based on your faith. He expects the miraculous to occur in your life because he expects you to allow him the freedom to perform. He expects you to be humbled as you learn more of him, to admit your need as you learn more about yourself, and to turn to your Father for guidance, healing, strength, and all of your needs. God expects you to love abundantly, but find that abundance within your soul—unaffected by your environment.

BOTTOM LINE

You will never please God by simply *doing* anything. You can only please God by allowing him to change your *being*. Then, and only then, will doing the right thing for the right reasons in the right way ever occur. What are you trying to do under your own power? What sins are you trying to overcome? What goals are you trying to accomplish? Stop. Do you recognize your need for God? Have you failed enough yet? Do you recognize how your expectations and desires limit the freedom that God has to provide? Relinquish anything but your need and appreciation for God's love and power. Ask for faith. Receive faith. Act on faith. Be changed. And live abundantly.

TALK TO GOD:

Quiet your mind. Read a short Psalm, maybe Psalm 100. Think about your idea of what a *good Christian* is and what a *good Christian* does. Spend time telling God how you are trying to "do" your faith. In what areas are you not trusting God to change, grow, or free you? Ask for help in giving up your efforts of doing and learning to trust more.

 DIG DEEPER:

Search the book of Matthew for the word *faith* and look at it in context of what Jesus is saying in the passage. What observations can you make about Jesus' view of faith and God's response to it?

Question 19

"What Can I Know?"

*My purpose is that they may be encouraged in heart
and united in love, so that they may have the full riches of
complete understanding, in order that they may know the
mystery of God, namely, Christ, in whom are hidden
all the treasures of wisdom and knowledge.*

Colossians 2:2–3

When I was a child, we had one special tradition: opening a single Christmas present of our choice on Christmas Eve. My siblings and I were usually so focused on Christmas Day that we forgot about this annual rite of the holiday until it was upon us. I believe the tradition was born simply out of the frustration my mother experienced when our incessant whining, present-shaking, late night peeking, and guessing reached a fever pitch. Looking back, it was a great ploy to get us to shut up and go to bed; but I believe she eventually received as much joy in the giving as we did in the receiving. Interesting, though, was the simultaneous awakening of a heightened degree of excitement equally accompanied by a quietness and gentle calm. We were happy. We had a peek into the glories to come and we slept.

The Christmas joy of a five-year-old is a pale comparison to eternity with God, but what else could even come close? Would the day you marry, have your first child, win the lottery, land the great job, or retire be an apt parallel? The Bible tells us that we will spend eternity in such amazement that every time we look at God's glory, we will fall to our faces in awe.

Face to face with God, our knowledge of him complete and perfect—that is the Christmas Day promise we will experience in eternity. But God has also given us a glimpse of the heavenly on the eve of our eternity. In fact, because our new nature is now that of Christ's, our eternity has essentially already begun—we are living our Christmas Eve. There's no need to wait until we die to experience God in his glory. "All" his glory will have to wait, but he desires to let us open whatever gifts of truth we can accept while walking this planet; and that is more than you might expect.

Just beware of the thief! This thief is your idea of who God is based on your past and current knowledge of him. Right now your idea is largely incorrect, and it will always be wrong to some degree because it will always be incomplete. This thief would rob you of the delight in knowing more about God. If knowing God is Christmas then giving up the pursuit of knowing God is the Grinch! There is so much you can know about God this side of eternity. Focusing on the knowable truths changes everything. That's when this deeper freedom can own your life. That's when you finally learn to see yourself as God sees you, which first requires that you know God a bit better. It changes everything when you see God the way he wants to be known, and he allows you to see others with his eyes. I pray we never discover the blessings we missed on earth—the gifts left unopened. The more you learn of God's character and unparalleled love, the more you will begin to wait expectantly for the Christmas Eve peek. Guess what ... Christmas Eve is every day! Learn to expect it; look forward to it. The mature Christian expects amazing blessings in both good times and bad. That's a perspective born of a knowledge of God and self that proves unshakable. Neither moves in storm or celebration. That's a perspective every Christian should have.

BOTTOM LINE

God wants to be known by you—intimately known—but you can only take a little at a time. Why? Because every time we see more of him, we see ourselves more clearly. There's still some ugly stuff that controls our thoughts and actions even after salvation and that shows us our desperate need for God. Trust me, you only want a little of that truth at a time. God being mysterious and you being somewhat ignorant is a blessing. That way God can always remain bigger than our biggest ideas, which gives him the freedom to amaze us every day. I can only trust a God who is bigger than I can conjure in my own mind. Is that the God you want to trust? Is that the adventure you want for your life?

TALK TO GOD:

If you can, go somewhere in the open and sit. Noisy or loud doesn't matter—just get outside. Read Psalm 19 and then look around. Think about what you see in the sky, the ground, and in between. What do you feel— wind, warmth, rain, snow? Think about what you don't understand concerning the things you just observed. Now, talk to God about how little you understand of the world around you—how creation works; how the earth is suspended in space and turns perfectly every day; how the sun works; how life comes into people and why it leaves—anything. Now tell him what you do know about the character of the Creator of the universe. What else do you want to know? Continue the conversation as you are led.

 # DIG DEEPER:

Read as much of Job 38–42 as you can in the time you have. Although known by God as blameless, upright, and unique among men, Job questioned God. What do you question about God's power and goodness? Is your response to the truth of God similar to Job's?

Question 20

"Why Do Bad Things Still Happen?"

"But the Scripture declares that the whole world is a prisoner of sin, so that what was promised, being given through faith in Jesus Christ, might be given to those who believe."

Galatians 3:22

She looked awful. Those red eyes, her rubbed-off makeup, and that blank, sad stare made it pretty obvious that she had been crying. Denise, this normally vibrant and happy young woman who could not only light up rooms with her smile but could illuminate entire city blocks, had collapsed in a heap of dark, musty sadness.

An hour or so passed as I tried to help her figure out the serious problems concerning her relationship with her boss, and how to confront a dreadfully uncomfortable issue, but she just kept getting more and more frustrated. Finally, it became evident that she wasn't so much upset about that particular situation; rather, her mind was occupied with a much larger concern.

"Why does it have to be this way? Why do people have to act the way they do? It's awful. The world is a disgusting place. Why do I have to deal with this kind of filth? I didn't do anything to deserve this. It's just not right."

Just two days later, at the same table, having dinner with a different friend, the conversation turned to plans for the future, and Ishmael suddenly grew bitter. In the last few months, fascist skinheads (a group of racists that regularly terrorize foreigners) had made his life a living nightmare. Skinheads had recently murdered his best friend in broad daylight. They had threatened Ishmael in a coffee shop and attacked two other friends so viciously that they required hospitalization. Another friend may have suffered permanent brain damage as the result of yet another skinhead attack. Each attack came from a different group. Some attacks were rather organized; others were random acts of hatred by drunkards. All were intended to incite fear.

Ishmael wanted to stay and continue at the university in Eastern Europe. His family, fearing for his life, refused to continue supporting him. Again, assuming his issue was localized to the immediate problem of safety and hatred toward his people group, I tried to search for solutions. As the conversation progressed, though, it was revealed that the root of his anger was not so much directed at his attackers, but was a much larger, philosophical issue.

"I hate being Arab. I wish someone would drop a bomb on the entire Middle East and wipe us all out. I can go almost nowhere without being accosted by the police. It is almost impossible to get a visa to study abroad in any country. But I guess that it shouldn't be a surprise. There is so much evil in the world, so much hatred. Why does it have to be this way? Why is everyone always fighting and hurting each other?"

What do you say to that? He was right. The world is a disgusting place.

But there is also another truth. The world is not alone, and the world is not in charge of you any longer.

Have you ever painted a room or hallway in your home, thinking that one little touch would make a nice improvement? Maybe you've lived in a new house for a few years and it is time to add a dash of color or spruce up the most heavily used area. Of course, you paint the room that needs it the most and maybe think it is the only one that needs any work at all. That is, until you get that beautiful, defect-free coat of paint up and finished.

After you clean up all the painting supplies and carefully put them away, you stop to admire your handiwork. Then your heart sinks a little. It is suddenly difficult to enjoy this new beauty. In the light of this wall of perfection, the neighboring wall that once looked okay, even nice, now appears filthy and in need of great repair. So you get out your brushes and ladder and start again, only to discover the same problem every time. One room leads to another, to another, and another, until either all the rooms get painted or you come to a section of your home that is well separated from the freshly painted areas.

"Whew, I'm finally done!"

Then you look down. The carpet! Agggggghhhhhh!!!!!

When you were cleaned white as snow from your sins

through the saving grace of God, you didn't stop sinning, but you stopped being a sinner. Your identity changed to that of Christ's brother or sister—his equal in inheritance with God. You are part of a new family, with a new name and a new identity. You are no longer a part of the family of sinners. Sure, you look pretty much the same, but there is a new nature inside of you and that's why your feelings and perspective make you more sensitive to the issue of right and wrong. God is disgusted by sin and you have God's heart. Therefore, you will be disgusted by sin, too.

You are correct: the world is not supposed to be this way, but it is, and it will be until the world as we know it ends. That very briefly explains your frustration with the way things are, but it doesn't address the "why." The "why" is a bit more complicated. If God loves you, how can bad stuff happen in the world and more specifically to you and those you love?

God gave man free will because that is the greatest love possible. He wants to be loved in a genuine way, which can't happen if he solved all of our problems like a genie in a bottle or if he took away all the bad in the world or forced people to love him. How can you force anyone to love you, anyway? If you tried, their response would be a lie; and your love would be more selfish and abusive than anything good and caring.

Nope, the only way a love relationship can be genuine is if both parties freely choose the other. Therefore, to be a choice, there must be an alternative. Choosing God is deciding you want to be freed from the eternal impact of all sin. Then God can see you as pure and be in loving relationship with you. Then he can perfect you in respect to your behavior and your tendency to continue to sin every day. No Christian gets this all right all the time, but throughout a lifetime, there should clearly be progress made in one's character and behavior as there is progress made in one's faith.

What's the opposite of that? Well, the people who choose not to believe and trust in Jesus Christ will exhibit differing degrees of sinful, hurtful, fearful, selfish, and angry behavior—just to mention a few. For relationship with God to be a choice, man must be subject to influences other than God. There is evil in the world, and if it were not for the grace of God, we might be willing participants in it.

This could really get you down if you didn't understand the rest of the story. God's willingness to allow evil to exist does not in any way imply that God is powerless or desires to hide His power. God's ultimate desire is to be glorified—since we were made for that purpose, we are most fulfilled when living within that purpose. For God to be glorified, he must be evident on earth.

So, if God is strong, then he is most evident when we are weak. If God is loving, he is most evident when someone is unlovable. If God is forgiving, he is most evident when someone needs to be forgiven greatly.

We can look at difficult situations as unfortunate. We can whine and complain. We can cry and yell at God. We can get angry and frustrated. We can become bitter and lash out. We can hide and avoid the world.

And when we are done with all that, what?

When my nephew, Connor, was just a couple of years old, we often sat in front of the big chalkboard I bought him for Christmas. After we "became artists" by painting chalk on each other's noses (our secret ritual that confounded his father for quite some time), he would grab a piece of chalk and feverishly scribble something on the board. I had no idea what he thought he was drawing, but there was always some form, some small shape that showed promise to a creative eye. I would then take my chalk in hand and turn a simple zigzag into a path up a huge mountain; or a lop-sided circle into a ball on a seal's nose; or some semblance of a triangle into a two story house with a door and walkway and little Connor peeking out the window.

Something simple, confusing, random, unformed, and even sometimes rather angry-looking was in actuality just the beginning of something wonderful and beautiful. After just a time or two, Connor began to get excited to see what would happen next. What would his uncle create out of the little thing he did? What great masterpiece was hidden inside the scribble?

Evil will continually lash out in the world regardless of how you feel about it; and because you will constantly bump up against it, you will forever be pushed and bruised and cut and torn. The real question is not "why evil," but "who is God." Does the evil in the world change the reality of the unchangeable God? The Bible tells us "in all things God works for the good of those who love him, who have been called according to his purpose" (Rom. 8:28). Do you look for God in the bad stuff or blame God for the choices of man and the forces of nature? Do you see difficulty as a wonderful opportunity for God to be glorified as he exerts his power or refines your character?

Pain hurts and it is good to mourn and be honest with your feelings. God is sad about sin, so you should be as well. And often your path to healing leads straight through the understanding of what's behind your emotions, so hiding them serves no good purpose.

BOTTOM LINE

Grace and love freed you to see all things from the grander perspective of the Creator of the Universe. If God is all powerful and all loving, the most awful thing you can think of can be made into a beautiful masterpiece that *gives* joy instead of *takes* it. Do you desire God to be glorified above all? The greater the darkness, the more vividly his light will shine. Can you see him? If not, call to him, and follow that voice to find a new perspective. Live as a free person. Don't allow the prison that traps the world to confine you ever again.

 TALK TO GOD:

Think on these perfect attributes of God that have no limit: *unchanging, loving, all-powerful, wise, just, merciful, uncompromising, good, full of grace.* Read Philippians 4:4–9 and ask God to help you understand more of him and see what good he desires to happen in you within the midst of pain and turmoil.

DIG DEEPER:

Make a list of your enemies. If that is too strong a
word for you, make a list of the people that do bad
things that hurt you or others you care about. Read
Luke 6:20–42. Think about what selfish or hurtful
things you were capable of doing before Christ was a
personal reality to you. Pick one person who is not
kind to you and resolve to act as Christ requests. Don't
give up. Do this regardless of their response. Through
time, you will see your own attitude toward them
change, and possibly even their attitude toward you.
Be patient. This may take months or years, but it can
actually become fun.

Question 21

"What Does Trusting God Look Like?"

"Now it is God who has made us for this very purpose and has given us the Spirit as a deposit, guaranteeing what is to come. Therefore we are always confident and know that as long as we are at home in the body we are away from the Lord. We live by faith, not by sight."

2 Corinthians 5:5–7

It is amazing the faith people have. Any day of the week, you can travel to a large city that isn't currently in a war of some sort and observe thousands of people walking down the street acting as though they will not be shot, robbed, or attacked from behind. Millions of people every day get on airplanes to fly long distances and drive cars onto crowded highways not thinking of imminent death. You push a button in an elevator or pick up a telephone without wondering if it will work.

People, complete strangers to you, are the critical component of these everyday experiences. For numerous reasons we trust them. Why?

It is recklessness, ignorance, deceit, or knowledge that leads one to trust.

If we are reckless, we are foolish. We don't count the costs, don't gather enough knowledge to make an informed decision, or don't care about the outcome. Fools will be hurt.

We can be ignorant of what it takes to make a good decision and not ask the right questions, seek the right counsel, or understand the process to become informed. The ignorant will be frustrated.

We can be deceived about the reality of what is good and most beneficial. If we receive wrong information, but follow a good process, we will be destined to failure. The deceived will be disappointed.

The knowledgeable are informed of truth gathered through a healthy process of research, personal discovery, outside counsel, and situational affirmation. They walk in confidence and live in complete freedom within the boundaries provided by what they know to be true. The knowledgeable find freedom to live to the fullest.

All of these statements are true, but there is something else required for all of them—everyone must *choose* to trust. If you choose not to decide, you still have made a choice. If you choose *not* to trust, you will reap the results of that choice, good or bad. It is just as important to not trust in the wrong thing as it is to trust in the right one. The path to trusting God is through knowledge of him, but there is a bit of a chicken and egg thing going on. Trust begets knowledge begets trust.

You can learn to make informed, intelligent, well-counseled decisions, but sometimes God doesn't appear to be logical because he has plans that extend beyond our available knowledge and understanding. If you are feeling a leading from God through prayer and reading, have sought counsel from godly people you trust, and have seen circumstances (or coincidences) that lead you to believe God may be at work, the next step is to check your motives and the impact of such an outcome.

You must determine if you are manipulating the situation in your mind or desiring to trust God completely.

To understand if what you do is *faith-based* or *you-based,* ask:

Who gets the credit?

Why did I do it?

Did my faith grow? Or will it be required to grow?

If God is the one who receives the credit, you did it because of the desire for God to be honored, and your understanding and knowledge of the truth of God grew because you were forced to trust in God to see it accomplished—then it was done in faith. This is biblical trust. This is the way Jesus trusted God when he was facing death. He didn't want it, even asked to get out of it, but he trusted that God's plan was good in the long run. Trusting God is never about you being honored, although that outcome is not out of the question. This is tricky to understand at first.

Trust also isn't about what people say and think, it is about what gives you peace within your heart. This kind of peace comes from the motives of your heart—the "Why did I do it?" Think of a desire you have for your future. What do you desire? Are you trusting God with it or trusting in your own abilities to make it happen? Another way to ask this question might be "Will I be content if no one besides God ever knows about it?" Trust is the certainty that ultimately God is in control of both the process and the outcome. It's not about you— it's about him. Sometimes God asks us to trust in ways that go far beyond our current comfort zone. You may have absolutely no frame of reference for what God is asking you to do—that is when you have to fall back on the truths you know about him and his character. If you are dependent on God to accomplish something, then your faith will grow, God will be honored, and whatever happens to you and your task is put into perspective.

Trusting God is as much about motive as it is about faith. You may believe God is capable, but you remain impatient; or maybe you desire to do it yourself and purposefully choose independence. Either way you must ask yourself why. Odds are, in every situation you face, there is something in your faith that needs to be strengthened, something to relinquish control of, or something to wait on to help you grow in wonder and amazement.

BOTTOM LINE

We reach a point in our knowledge and experience where there's little risk involved in trusting. It's the unknown and unfamiliar that requires a greater degree of trust. With God, there is never a risk. The more you know and experience him, the easier it will be for you to embrace that truth. Until then, you must make the choice to trust him.

Talk to God:

Have you broken trust with someone in your life? Did they break trust? What will or what did it take to reconcile? Now turn your attention to God and consider that in his perfect love he never broke trust with you and never will. Tell Jesus what you think about the great desire he has for you to be in relationship with him, free of all fears, full of trust and love. Now, can you trust God to help you reconcile a difficult relationship? Will you allow yourself to be humbled in the process and give as Christ gave for you, without expectation of anything in return?

 # Dig Deeper:

Read Romans 4 and consider what Paul says about faith. Where does faith come from? What does faith lead us to do? What are the benefits of faith? Why do some not have faith? What kind of faith do you have?

Question 22

"What Is Sin?"

"Search me, O God, and know my heart; test me and know my anxious thoughts. See if there is any offensive way in me, and lead me in the way everlasting."

Psalm 139:23–24

I know you've eagerly anticipated this section of the book. It's one of the greatest desires of all would-be godly people—the list of sins to avoid. Lucky for you, your wait is over! To guarantee that you will be a good Christian, the best possible Christian, I've compiled a list of all the things you can and can't do to make sure your life will always be pleasing in God's sight:

Good news! You can dance—but like King David did in the Old Testament (2 Sam. 6:14), not like they do on MTV. Oh, and no dancing at all for the person who had negative experiences in bars before becoming a Christian and who might have bad memories triggered that could lead her to sin. She probably shouldn't even watch other people dance—that is, until she is more spiritually mature and has effectively dealt with her sin patterns. Okay, she can go to the ballet. That's different; she can watch that kind of dancing. Maybe she shouldn't touch another guy while dancing … well, until she's sixty-five and retired and learns ballroom dancing—because that's not dirty, although they touch—and, well, she's retired and it is great exercise and fun, and it would be with her husband. Yeah, dancing with your husband when you are elderly is okay, but not before. Dancing is solely for the married, old and decrepit, or the professional ballerina. Is that clear?

Well, that covers dancing, now let's look at the Internet.

You can surf any site on the Internet except sites that promote or show nudity, sex, gambling, profanity, or anything detestable. Well, except for that person who has a history with Internet pornography and hasn't addressed the issues behind it. That person probably shouldn't use the Internet at all or at least not in private. But he can do it for his job if he doesn't work at home. It would also be okay if he did it alone in his office during the day, but not at night alone in his office. After all, he has to get his work done and can't pay someone to observe him all day. That would be creepy. As for the person who works for greater legislative control of what's on the Internet, he can visit some of those sites for research, as well as the people who create web site filters for family access because they provide a great service. Those people may have to visit reprehensible sites occasionally and that would be all right, I guess. And as far as the nudity part goes, no pornography sites, but you can visit the museum websites and look at pictures of famous nude sculptures, but only if you are doing research for a school paper or something, because why else would you want to ... I mean, really? And it would be okay because they aren't real people, although they were created from real models. But, then again, photos aren't real people, but were taken of real people; and some photos are certainly sexually suggestive, but the people are fully clothed. Hmmmmm. Maybe you should just stay away from the Internet altogether.

Well, those are the rules on the Internet. Let's look at drinking alcohol instead—or better yet, going to bars. That's a simple one.

Okay, bars: don't go in them. Well, actually, I know of several churches that meet in bars because they are closed on Sundays and have great equipment for services and sit in the very neighborhoods of the people the church wants to reach. That would be okay, if it is a church. So, maybe it is best to not go in a bar if they are serving alcohol, but okay if they aren't. But some churches, like the Vatican, serve wine for communion, but he's the Pope and you might just be a tourist, and, well, this drinking issue is just too controversial to discuss. Oh, yeah, and the recovering alcoholic—he can't go into a bar at all, even if it is a church, because of the smell triggers. In fact, he probably shouldn't even ride down the street where the bar is, if he has a history there—unless he has successfully overcome that sin trigger. Well, sometimes it would be okay if he were feeling strong, since it is the shortest way home, but on a weak day, like when he's depressed or angry, he shouldn't ride down that street. But you can. That would be just fine.

I think that just about does it. Is all that clear? Do we need to talk about sin anymore? Have you got it all figured out?

Now, go and sin no longer.

Yeah, right. That didn't help much, did it?

Sin ought to be easy to figure out, but it isn't so clear-cut, is it? What's right? What's wrong? Is sin subjective? Is my sin different than your sin? We've got the Ten Commandments, but the likelihood of you murdering someone, or even requiring a list to tell you it is a bad thing, is pretty remote. Anyone who needs a list to tell them that murder is wrong is probably already sitting on death row somewhere.

We need a longer list, more detailed. Maybe we should create a list of the 100 or 1000 or 10,000 commandments. Then, if we could keep those, we would be good Christians and God would be happy with us. We would know just what to do.

That's exactly what was going on during Christ's time on earth. That's exactly what was going *wrong* during Christ's time on earth. The very tools, these lists of sins, supposedly designed to lead all people closer to God, created a diversion from honoring God.

The religious leaders of that time, the Pharisees and Sadducees, valued the list of sins and righteous acts above all and made their attitudes—not God's—the object of aspiration. They so devoutly worshiped *the list* that they completely missed the glory of God, even when they were standing face to face. Christ took exception to the list and led others to follow his example; not just because he was God, but because he was also man and desired to show us how to *choose* with God's direct influence and not just follow the example of other men.

When Christ went against the desires of the religious leaders, they accused him of sinning. Of course, they didn't accept that Jesus, being God, could not sin. Many of these acts of supposed sin by the only sinless man ever—sins like healing people on the wrong days, speaking to God in a familiar tone, touching the sick, and not ceremonially washing before dinner—are the real reasons they placed him on that cross. If he followed someone else's list without question, he wouldn't have been God, and he wouldn't have lived as God intends a man to live.

You may look at Christ's time as an extreme, but aren't we often acting as those religious leaders? If you look closely enough, you may see yourself or organizations and individuals you respect in their reflection, regardless of their good intentions. We tend to think of sin as something wrong that we do, but we also sin when we know the right thing to do and choose not to do it. Sin separates us from God and *his* intentions for our lives.

God doesn't desire us to merely act properly according to some predetermined criteria for everyday living. No list would ever be sufficient. No list could ever be followed. God desires us to think as he thinks, to know as he knows, and to choose as he chooses out of a changed heart and inspiration from his Spirit. Although there were absolutes that Christ never strayed from—and so we shouldn't—the gray areas abounded, just like today. Christ looked at each situation and made the perfect, most appropriate choice for the moment.

BOTTOM LINE

Only God's definition of sin matters. He can give the power to resist sin and has the power to forgive sin. So it just makes sense to go to the source for the answer to the sin question. How can you access this source? First, read the Bible. God has a lot to say about sin in it. Second, depend on the Holy Spirit within you to teach you about sin. The question facing you is "How do I understand what is sin?"

TALK TO GOD:

Sit in front of a mirror and get comfortable in case you will be there for a long time. Look at yourself. What do you see? Don't rush this time. Take it seriously. What emotions begin to well up as you stare at yourself? Who are you, really? Do you see your identity as defined by your failures or successes, appearance, or emotions? Ask God how he sees you. Thank him for freeing you from the eternal impact of your sin, and ask him to reveal what is in you that leads you to continue to sin. Now ask him for help to identify and be protected from the steps that lead to sin.

 ## DIG DEEPER:

Read James 4:17 and think about what you know you ought to do but don't. Are you trusting God with it, or not involving him? Do you want freedom from it or are you trusting that sin to provide some form of perceived freedom. What do you know is a lie? What is truth? What does the Bible say? What is God telling you he wants to do for you? What's your next step?

Question 23

"When Does Sin Begin?"

> *My son, pay attention to my wisdom, listen well to my*
> *words of insight, that you may maintain discretion and*
> *your lips may preserve knowledge. For the lips of an adulteress*
> *drip honey, and her speech is smoother than oil; but in the end she*
> *is bitter as gall, sharp as a double-edged sword ... Keep to a path*
> *far from her, do not go near the door of her house.*

> *Proverbs 5:1–4, 8*

Maureen was back after sixteen years, but it was far from a happy reunion for either party. Maureen, an alcoholic, was walking through the doors of the same rehabilitation facility that helped her get back on track so long ago. The pit in her stomach began to boil. This was her first relapse. Life threw some curveballs last year, and this time she was unable to resist. It wasn't that these difficulties were considerably more painful than previous years when she was able to stay dry; it was just that they happened when her defenses were down and strength limited. To hear her tell it, with newfound clear-headed hindsight, she was more susceptible to the pull of sin because she had been courting it for a year.

As an alcoholic, Maureen knew that drinking alcohol even in the slightest quantity wasn't an option, but after awhile she didn't see the harm in ancillary indulgences. After more than a decade clean, she longed for the feel of a champagne glass and the taste of a beer. She didn't see the harm in enjoying a little sparkling apple cider in a tall, crystal flute or non-alcoholic beer in a frosty mug. For months, this provided a momentary, occasional distraction, but soon she looked forward to coming home to relax with a "near beer" during the evening news every night. In fact, she began to think about that frosty mug at lunch. Still faithfully attending her AA meetings, she felt impervious to completely stepping over the line of sobriety. She had too much to lose. Sixteen years sober, three kids, and a loving husband seemed plenty to motivate her continued dry life.

That is, until those curveballs came fast and furious and the thought of an escape, however temporary, became quite appealing. One non-alcoholic beer became three, three became a real Budweiser, and one real beer became twelve. One day, she woke up in a pool of despair and disgust on a random bench after binging at the airport bar, her temporary coma causing her to miss her flight to rehab. As if being forced by her husband to return to rehab wasn't embarrassing enough, now she had to let him know, in a drunken stupor, that she had missed her connecting flight.

Maureen knew all along, without the slightest doubt, that

drinking alcohol was a sin for her. Until that moment, she hadn't realized the reach of that sin. Now she realized, a little late, that sin for an alcoholic began long before alcohol passed her lips.

Sin is like that: one leads to another, to another. It's much like a tiny crack in a dam. At first there's no real concern, but the pressure created by the built-up force behind that small point of release begins to stretch that crack. Sin is insatiable. When it smells freedom, just a little crack of light to sneak through, it jams a crowbar in the hole and invites its friends— its larger friends, the ones that can't fit through the tiny hole but are big enough to knock out enough chunks—to pass through standing.

I once chose to take a leisurely stroll down the path of the "innocent" sin and found myself in a fast car on a sixteen-lane interstate before I knew what happened. I now know there are three things you must discover about your sin to overcome it.

What need are you trying to fulfill on your own outside of trusting God?

What triggers this need?

How can you trust God to heal that need and protect you in the process?

It is the triggers to sin you must avoid. If you are concentrating on avoiding the sin, you're too late. What makes you sin? What is inside you that cries out for something harmful? What do you not believe about God and his ability to satisfy? What do other people see in you that you have trouble recognizing? What do you not allow them to see?

Sin begins in the mind before it moves to action. You won't usually set out to harm yourself or others or grieve God, but that is the end result of sin. You need to examine your choices: is that little choice you make that sometimes leads to sin beneficial? Is the choice, this little thing, helping you understand God better? Do you desire to thank God for the experience in the midst of it, or would you prefer to not think about God?

BOTTOM LINE

You don't need to become a prude, but you must become fully aware of what drives you, what compels you, and where you need healing. Deny this truth and you will surely live in despair and guilt. Throw open those doors, air those rooms, and bring in the light of the Son, and you can live in freedom and joy.

 TALK TO GOD:

Now is the time for confession. Tell God something secret. Confess an emotion, action, or desire that you are ashamed of. Ask for freedom from that and for a greater desire for purity. Ask for help to find greater pleasure in the knowledge of God and in trusting him than in fulfilling your own desires in your own way.

 DIG DEEPER:

Read Proverbs 5 and think about what "snares" exist in your life and how to avoid them. Talk to a friend and share each other's snares and discuss how you can help each other.

Question 24

"Who Is Satan and Why Should I Care?"

As for you, you were dead in your transgressions and sins, in which you used to live when you followed the ways of this world and of the ruler of the kingdom of the air, the spirit who is now at work in those who are disobedient.

Ephesians 2:1–2

"The devil made me do it."

We've all heard that quick quip spoken in jest to justify a minor indiscretion and deflect responsibility, but we don't really believe it, do we? I mean, really, do you honestly believe that there are a bunch of demons running about whispering in your ear in an attempt to trip you up and pull you from God's arms? Adults are too mature to believe in that, aren't they? Is it absurd to believe in a being you can't see, who has intentions and a plan for your life, and who wants to guide you to live a certain way for his own benefit? It's just plain silly, right? You say you believe in God? Why is it that we are willing to accept the idea of God, who is spirit and invisible, but not his opposite? Why is it easier to believe that there are only good forces in the spirit world that influence us?

Whatever good God desires for you to experience, a battle ensues to get you there. In the book of Revelation at the end of the Bible, the book that describes the ending of man's time on earth, Satan is described as a hideous red dragon waiting to devour. There is much to study about this former angel who fell from God's grace and took a third of God's angels with him—this fallen angel who is forever dedicated to ruling on earth and battling against God until Christ takes complete control. None of that knowledge much matters at the end of the day unless you understand one thing deep in your soul: the primary thing that matters is that you believe Satan exists and he wants to destroy your relationship with God.

If you believe in God and the need to have Christ in your life with his spirit ruling your heart, you must, I repeat, must, believe in a counter spirit who is in a constant battle for that same piece of real estate. If you do not believe that, nothing really makes much sense. It would make no sense why God would create us perfect, but with free will to reject him (why, then, would we ever choose to reject him?). It would make no sense why we would need a savior at all if there were not an evil influence that separated us from God.

Believe it. Trust it. And understand that he didn't go very far. In fact, he's angry that he was evicted from your heart and he wants back in. Satan may be outside the place that Christ has made his home, but you can still hear him in the street. He knocks on the door and begs you to leave the safety of that place and join him. He entices you with smells and sounds from the street below. He pipes his messages into your heart electronically and mails you invitations daily. He attempts to infiltrate Christ's home—your heart—with every tool at his disposal. His is a battle of lies, but he does not advertise his identity. In fact, he would mostly prefer that you did not even believe he existed at all.

Think about it. What would you do if you were in his shoes? What would you do if the person you wanted to influence knew perfectly well that you were evil and you wanted them to not only accept you, but to even trust completely in you—in fact, to worship you? What would you do if your adversary was all-powerful, all good, all loving, completely honest, and in every way your enemy? What strategies would you use to accomplish your objective?

A straightforward approach would only work with those who were angry with God, so you could only truly reveal your intention and identity to a handful of people. For those who didn't really believe in God or Jesus, you could easily make your mark by being completely invisible and just giving them what they want. After all, once man (i.e., Adam) turned from God, all of us were born with a sinful heart.

I got a sad but revealing picture of the sinful nature of man from my nephew when he was less than two years old. With only a vocabulary of a few words, he had a grasp of "no" more than most and used it quite often. One day he was instructed specifically not to do something by his mother as she was walking out of the room. I sat in the next room as he thought about it, made a choice, and disobeyed. A few minutes later, his mother confronted him and asked if he did it.

I observed as he thought about the dilemma he now found himself in. He had a choice to make, and he lied—consciously, purposefully, lied. He didn't lie because he hadn't been properly nurtured; he didn't lie because of social influences. He chose in his heart to do the wrong thing all by himself.

What led me to Christ was a desire for change in my heart, for forgiveness of all the bad things I had done, but I didn't really know how that would impact my future. I know now that all too often I still can choose to do the wrong thing. No matter how much I want to do what's right, I'm faced with the weight of a choice every time. So are you. Everyone is born with that same sinful, rebellious nature my nephew exhibited—everyone! If you have accepted Christ, you are no longer the same person, but you might still do many of the same things. What has happened is that your lord, your king to whom you are subject, has changed. Christ now fills that role, so you take on his identity. The Evil One, however, has not been eliminated. Both God and Satan still exist in your life—just as they always have. The difference is that they have changed position. Satan, no longer in the supreme role, lurks on the outside, looking for any opportunity to regain influence.

Think about traveling throughout Europe in medieval times. Whatever land you lived in, you were subject to the lord of that land. When Satan was thrown out of heaven, he became lord of this world. As long as you lived in his land, Satan had influence over you. Then Jesus came into the picture. He stormed the gates and overthrew the lord of this world. Now he has invited you to join him in rallying a rebellion against the occupying lord. You made a choice that you wanted a new lord and trusted that being the subject of Jesus was the right choice.

Jesus took over, but he didn't kill Satan—he banished him. So, when Satan enters the land, it is as an outlaw. He defies Jesus at every opportunity. He's angry and desires to undermine Jesus' authority. He invites you to join his rebellion, but when you refuse, you become his enemy, too.

So, Satan runs about in the shadows of the land, mugging unsuspecting travelers: good folk, who want to do the right thing, but occasionally find themselves in the wrong place at the wrong time. Sometimes they are lured away from the safety of their true Lord, from the lighted streets and protecting authority he provides, and they travel down a dark alley. At times, they willfully choose to go back to the ways they knew for so many years before he came along. The past is more familiar and comfortable than this new life, and whenever they begin to think that way, their old evil lord whispers lies of affirmation from behind the mask that hides his true identity.

This is a perpetual battle until we die. If you choose to deny the existence of the battle or its combatants, you will wander around without consideration for your safety. You will be unaware and you will lose the battle. And, if you choose to fight the battle on your own, you will be overtaken. You will lose, even with the best of intentions.

BOTTOM LINE

You must remember that you have a Lord who rules your heart and has committed to protect it from intruders so that you can live in peace. The battle isn't yours. You must identify the enemy, live in awareness of his plans, and arm yourself against him. Then trust in your Lord to win the battle. This is a choice. It is a choice you will make every day of your life to some degree.

 ## TALK TO GOD:

Thank Jesus for being the Lord of your heart. Ask him for discernment to choose well today and sensitivity to understand what urges and leadings are from him and what are against him. Ask God to block the power of Satan in your life when you are tempted—at the moment it is occurring.

 ## DIG DEEPER:

Go find a breeze either outside or inside. What do you see? How do you know the wind is moving? Now think about the spiritual world. Look at Ephesians 6:10–12. How can you recognize Satan's movements? How do you recognize God moving in your life?

Question 25

"Should I Get Baptized?"

Then Jesus came from Galilee to the Jordan to be baptized by John. But John tried to deter him, saying, "I need to be baptized by you, and do you come to me?"

Jesus replied, "Let it be so now; it is proper for us to do this to fulfill all righteousness." Then John consented.

Matthew 3:13–15

Dunking, sprinkling, child baptism, blah, blah, blah …

Lots of religious people argue about stuff like baptism and the right way or the wrong way to do this or that, but I think they miss the point. The issue isn't how, or when, or even so much about why—but why not?

We've talked about the purpose for which you, and all mankind for that matter, were created: to be in a healthy relationship with God, which requires an ever-increasing knowledge of him. So, if that is the point of life, then questions like baptism become pretty simple.

Why not be baptized? Christ was. Christ was an adult and completely without sin, but still chose to be baptized in the presence of other believers. He was identifying with the sin of all people and humbling himself to God. It was in stark contrast to the prideful religious leaders of the day. Christ chose to demonstrate his commitment to God and God chose to reveal himself through that experience. The heavens opened up, the Holy Spirit came down like a dove and landed on Christ's shoulder, and the crowd heard God say, "You are my Son, whom I love: with you I am well pleased."

Wow, how cool is that?

My baptism was much like that, sans dove and audible voice. It was multimedia, though, as I read a letter revealing my dark heart before I met Christ and then played a tape of the moment after I accepted Christ when I told Susan's answering machine the great news (twice ... it hung up on me once). I chose to go deep under the water and be completely covered. Was it the "right" way to do it? I didn't have a clue. All I knew at the time was that I wanted to know God more, and anything, ANYTHING that would allow me a glimpse into the experience of Christ shot to the top of the list.

God chose to reveal himself that day in much the same way as when Christ was baptized. Other people heard my story, saw my joy in publicly declaring my commitment to Christ, and were changed. One woman prayed to receive Christ that day. Another decided to be baptized. God was there. God spoke to the masses and he spoke to me. None of us was ever the same from that day forward. There was no doubt in my mind that God was pleased with me that day, and no doubt in the congregation's minds that I was very much pleased with God.

BOTTOM LINE

Lots of people disagree about the specifics of baptism, but don't get caught up in all that. All you need to do is ask yourself these two questions:

Is my faith real enough to want to publicly declare it?

Do I want to experience something that Christ experienced?

If yes, then what are you waiting for?

 TALK TO GOD:

Praise God for coming to earth in the form of a man, Jesus Christ, to show us the path to all righteousness and freedom from sin. Address God by a very personal name like daddy, dad, or papa. Does it feel weird? Ask him to give you opportunities to experience more of him and grow in your understanding of his heart and passions.

DIG DEEPER:

Talk to your church—or find one that you can trust—and ask what their requirements for baptism are. If they have a course, take it. If they require a discussion with a pastor or leader, sit down and have that talk. You don't have to choose at this time, but you should understand why you would or would not get baptized. If there is a real barrier to feeling totally free in making a public declaration of your faith, you must make that a priority to figure out.

Question 26

"Is My Path Unique?"

I keep asking that the God of our Lord Jesus Christ, the glorious Father, may give you the Spirit of wisdom and revelation, so that you may know him better. I pray also that the eyes of your heart may be enlightened in order that you may know the hope to which he has called you, the riches of his glorious inheritance in the saints, and his incomparably great power for us who believe.

Ephesians 1:17–19

"I don't want to become frumpy and boring. Is that what is required? Will God take away my passion and make me dull?"

Ginny was an exciting, passionate, smart, and funny person who was very much alive in every way. She liked herself and had a healthy view of life, but didn't see the same joy and boundless energy in other believers. She felt as though maybe she was living wrongly, but didn't like the idea of becoming something else—something she wasn't. Was that the path to maturity? She desperately desired to grow up in the likeness of Christ, to become the woman he desired her to be; but the idea of the passivity and quietness she saw in others was almost too much to bear. Not that it was wrong; it was just wrong for her.

Was there only one path to spiritual maturity? What was her responsibility along this path? Was it to change herself and her outlook and do what other people do or something else? Ginny sensed that God wanted something else for her, but she had not yet developed an ear for his voice. She had many questions in her first months following Christ, and she would have many more in years to come. To date, she relied on other people's interpretations of God's leading, but occasionally felt uncomfortable and possibly out of God's will in following their advice. It was time for her to step out of the shadow of her teachers and learn to talk to God herself, but that was very scary. They knew so much more than she. How could she make these choices herself?

One day, a close confidant and teacher did a very wise thing—she stopped answering Ginny's questions. She felt Ginny understood enough about God's desires and character and had found truth in the Bible, so she began to step out of the role of authority that Ginny had placed her in and directed Ginny to God. Every time Ginny asked what to do or how to act, the friend would ask her what she thought God would have to say about it; and then not offer an opinion. This wise leader taught her to discern the voice of God through Scripture, circumstance, and counsel, but to never rely on just one, and to always start with God. Ginny learned that she had primary responsibility for navigating her path and the fact that she needed to get good at that was the most important thing she could learn about herself.

You can only discover what maturity means for you by the active pursuit of God's character, guided by his Spirit, and through biblical truth and wise counsel from those who know you. Seek counsel from wise leaders, but value personal, Spirit-led discernment above all in your never-ending pursuit of truth. After all, the core of Christianity is about your relationship with God. You are the beautiful bride and Christ is the adoring groom. No person should ever come between that union or hold a position of greater authority than the total commitment of that relationship.

If you take time to think about this, it is actually more freeing than frightening to know that YOU have responsibilities in your quest for spiritual and emotional maturity. It means the life of a Christian is about personal discovery, personal enlightenment, and personal growth. It does not mean that because the God we worship has been known forever and the book we study is many centuries old, that the answers for your life are pre-defined. God's Spirit and Word are provided to assist you in finding your particular path, your unique purpose. God knows already, but he's not telling; well, at least not all at once.

BOTTOM LINE

Through study, prayer, counsel, and personal experience, your picture of God can become clearer every day—thus, your understanding of yourself and others will grow. That is precisely what leads to lasting heart change. Isn't it exciting to know that your life is designed to be completely unique and full of joyous adventure? Be yourself. Be Jesus Christ in YOU.

 TALK TO GOD:

Think of as many things as you can that are plentiful but perfectly unique (e.g., butterflies, fingerprints, sunsets, eyes, stars). Now think of lots of people you know and how different they are, but how they also share similarities. Thank God for all the things about you that are different. Praise him for his wisdom in making you who you are and leading you down your unique path.

 DIG DEEPER:

Read the first chapter of Genesis and circle every time God reflected on his creation. What is the same about you and God? What is different about you and other people you know? What is his opinion of his creation? Was your uniqueness a mistake? Is it logical that the Creator of the heavens and the earth and all that is in them makes mistakes? How do you think God wants you to look at yourself? How can he help you do just that?

Question 27

"Is God's Path Logical?"

"Follow my decrees and be careful to obey my laws, and you will live safely in the land. Then the land will yield its fruit, and you will eat your fill and live there in safety."

Leviticus 25:18–19

"My sheep listen to my voice; I know them, and they follow me."

John 10:27

I love the mountains and have spent countless days backpacking alone or in small groups, but my first desert excursion was an entirely different experience. Fortunately, my friend Jeff was quite experienced and adept at navigation. After several days being guided along a circuitous route without marked trails, spending most of our time knee deep in a river because the brush was so thick, we abruptly emerged on the edge of a huge desert in the midst of the Grand Staircase National Park in southern Utah. This is no flat desert like in the movies, but rather seemingly endless rolling mounds of solid rock surrounded by sand and the occasional scrub brush. It was nice to be out in the open.

Miles away in the distance, we could see the outline of the cliff where our car had rested the previous few days. It looked simple enough to get there, I thought, and much easier than mountain hiking since we could see our destination. There was no chance to get lost, so I boldly began hiking as the crow flies, dreaming of warm pizza, clean clothes, and a long hot shower.

Jeff, the experienced one who had hiked this terrain before, didn't budge. He was busy studying his topographical map and compass. *How silly*, I thought, *we're going right over there.* If I didn't know him better I might have thought he was becoming one of those perfectionist backpackers who must do everything by the book, forsaking fun and logic for perfection. I knew better. Jeff was not that kind of man. He was as laid back as they come, but he also did everything with a purpose. I realized that Jeff must know something I didn't, so I stopped, turned around, and waited for his experienced wisdom.

He showed me where we were and pointed to where we were going—due west. The car was due south. After a few hundred yards west, we went south a little ways, and then east, then south, then west, south again, and so on. We zig-zagged across this desert for most of the day, but after our first turn, I knew why.

Occasionally we tried a shortcut and took the obvious path, but realized after a few ascents that the smart path, the other one, was considerably less taxing. We soon became quite comfortable with addressing the best next step, seeking direction from our map and compass to ensure we moved in the right direction, and avoided the continual ups and downs. We tacked like a sailboat in a stiff wind and made the most of our environment.

Traveling the obvious, straight path was the hard road. It was full of ups and downs: climbing, descending, climbing, descending, over and over. The path we chose allowed us to keep our end goal in site by staying at as high and consistent an elevation as possible, descending only when there was no other way. In the end, we figured our weaving saved us about 20 percent in steps, probably two hours of hiking, and considerable energy. (This got me to a thick slice of pepperoni pizza that much earlier.)

I probably could have made it across the desert without dying, if I judged the effort well enough, brought adequate water, and avoided the dangerous little critters. Trusting my more experienced friend and following his lead made my trip not only doable, but also most enjoyable. Had I not heeded his direction, I certainly would have experienced more difficulty, danger, and perhaps the occasional fear.

Likewise, the path God has for you may not always be obvious. When it's not, he'll provide a guide, a map, and a compass. God is not logical, as you know logic. God has perfect wisdom, which means he has chosen the perfect destination and the best path. Is it the shortest? Most of the time it is not, because the destination isn't the only objective. The real objective is what changes in you along the way, which is dependent upon what you allow yourself to learn about God and yourself as you travel. If arrival at a particular place, for a particular thing, or in a particular time is your primary goal, you will be disappointed. God's in it for the journey—and the change in your heart the journey will bring.

BOTTOM LINE

Do you trust in God's wisdom? Will you allow him to direct your path illogically and have the confidence that you are better off? You must, or live a life of constant disappointment. Do you really want to follow a god that isn't any smarter than you are? Can you trust in a god that can't see further and wider than you? If you don't understand the end of the path or any step beyond the next one, you are in a wonderful place to grow in your spiritual maturity. Enjoy the walk, drink in the scenery, listen to the voice of the guy with the compass and follow his lead, and you will arrive rested and joyful.

 ## TALK TO GOD:

Think about whom you trust and why? Praise God for his wisdom and goodness that surpasses all human wisdom and goodness. Ask your Holy Father to help you grow in trust and faith.

 ## DIG DEEPER:

Read Psalm 111. Think about what of this Psalm you can believe in your own life and what you don't. Talk to another believer about what you discover.

Question 28

"What Is 'Fellowship'?"

And let us consider how we may spur one another on toward love and good deeds. Let us not give up meeting together, as some are in the habit of doing, but let us encourage one another—and all the more as you see the Day approaching.

Hebrews 10:24–25

I didn't know these people and they had no clue about me; but there I was sitting in the middle of a room with twenty or so total strangers praying for me. Most of them didn't even speak my language. I was a foreigner, an alien in someone else's land, surrounded by people with whom I had next to nothing in common. Why did they care so much for a stranger, and why did I so appreciate the fact that they did? Why did it impact me so deeply that I cried? Could it be I was made for this? Could it be that this common bond of Christ's Spirit is true everywhere, within all people in his family?

Fellowship—what a word. Where other than church do you ever hear that word? It's one of the official "Christian lingo" terms that is so often used within those circles that it actually starts sounding normal in time. It's such a foreign concept to the average un-churched person that you should probably avoid speaking it to anyone who isn't a confirmed believer or risk being marked a religious freak before they actually get to know you. Frankly, I never use the word, but don't much mind when others do.

This is the word that Christians use to describe the essence of the experience of being in a community of fellow Christ followers. As weird as the word may feel at first, the experience is something you will hopefully grow to appreciate a great deal. There is something powerful that happens when two or more people get together for the purpose of encouragement and honoring God.

This is a rare thing outside of church, which explains why the word is so uncommon in regular conversation. Any good friend can console you when you are hurting or offer advice when you have questions, but those friends are few and far between in the normal world. Can you imagine going to a meeting of total strangers in a foreign country and feeling perfectly at home? Is it difficult to imagine even being in a group of local friends and feeling completely free to express your fears, doubts, and even your failures?

Fellowship is that time of faith in action, of loving your brother, of considering someone else's needs more than your own. It's one of those remarkable times when you connect to God's heart and see him change lives—your life—the lives of people in need. Sometimes it's just hangin' out and feeling free to be yourself, sometimes it's crying a deep pool of hurt, but always fellowship is about love and acceptance in the context of a common faith in God. You may sometimes need to give it, sometimes get it; but it is certainly something you will want to take part in.

BOTTOM LINE

Just because the word is weird doesn't mean the experience should be. Being honest and real with other people will feel that way at first, but like the word, you may get so used to it that nothing else will say love like being with other believers.

 ## Talk to God:

Tell God about any hang-ups you have with hanging out with other Christians. Confess any prideful ideas that might be hindering you. Ask God to give you an opportunity to encourage another follower of Jesus without expecting anything in return. Ask him to open your heart to receive fellowship from other believers.

 ## Dig Deeper:

Are you meeting with other believers? If not, you need to find a church, attend a Bible study, or start meeting with someone every week for coffee. Take a chance to trust someone with the inside of your life—your spiritual parts.

Question 29

"Can I Do This Alone?"

All of you, clothe yourselves with humility toward one another,
because, "God opposes the proud but gives grace to the humble."
Humble yourselves, therefore, under God's mighty hand,
that he may lift you up in due time.

1 Peter 5:5–6

"I just don't see a need to go to church.
God and I are just fine together. I read my
Bible every day and pray. I don't need anyone
else involved. My relationship with God is a
personal thing and I want to keep it that way."

My friend, Jonathan, was quite adamant. Over the last year, in the midst of his depression and loneliness, he held fast to remaining independent. Over that same time, he changed, and not for the better. He became more withdrawn and depressed, and although he aged physically, he was more and more spiritually immature every day. It was quite remarkable actually, how the things he never questioned about God began to unravel a little every day. His faith was failing and there was nothing I could do to help.

This person who is so dear to me became disillusioned about the value of sharing his relationship with God with other followers of Jesus because some of those people disappointed him. They didn't reflect Christ as he decided they should, and he wrote off the lot of them. Sure, he saw how God used caring individuals in his life, but he never truly understood the value of the collective power of believers.

So what does all this humility stuff have to do with church? Well, if you knew Jonathan, you would also recognize that his unmet expectations of others reflected his unmet expectations of himself. What we see as the worst in others is often what they might see in us. If he had chosen to look inside and ask what God wanted to change, he would have allowed God to grow and mature him; but instead, he avoided God's revealing truth by avoiding other believers. Jonathan didn't like the idea of trusting in people who could hurt just as well as help. The idea of it pushed every fear button he had because it forced him to trust in something outside of man or himself. It forced him to trust in God—but God wouldn't force Jonathan's hand, so he remained separated from any community of believers (known in the Bible as the body of Christ).

It may sound odd to hear that I've known many people just like Jonathan who attend church every single week. Actually, Jonathan's choosing to not attend church is more honest than those who do attend and never break the plane of relationship and step into trust. Those people can go and go and go, but unless they develop meaningful relationships, ten years later they will likely not be much more mature than they were the very first day they walked in the door.

One of the earliest followers of Christ, Peter, says to be humble is a responsibility of the individual. In other words, personal development as a Christian lies first and foremost with each individual, but this cannot be adequately accomplished in isolation. Just as the employee who does not take advantage of the resources available to further her skills and personal development will be hindered in advancement in her career, the Christian who does not take ownership of his own development will slowly or never advance spiritually.

Nobody rides alone. This journey is ALL about relationship. It is therefore about experience and time, trials and celebrations, and learning truth and letting go of lies. It's about knowing a man named Jesus Christ and getting introduced to God, your daddy, discovering a little more each day. It's about getting to know yourself by spending time with God and other people that share his loving—and convicting—Spirit. Introvert or extrovert matters not; everything good about this Christian life is based in relationship.

BOTTOM LINE

God calls you into relationship with him and other people because our greatest fears, insecurities, weaknesses, and pride are rarely exposed in private. God is in relentless pursuit of peeling back those layers to uncover the pure heart hidden underneath that life of lies, and he's called in the army to help free the captives. You are called into community. It is a biblical and very logical mandate if you want to grow.

TALK TO GOD:

Read Philippians 1:6 and thank God for this promise.

 ## DIG DEEPER:

Make a list of the things you don't like about organized religion. Make a list about the things you desire in your relationship with God. Read Romans 15:1–13 and write down a description of the value of that group of believers to the spiritual growth of its members.

Question 30

"What Do I Need from Church?"

*Later when Jesus was eating supper at Matthew's house with his
close followers, a lot of disreputable characters came and joined
them. When the Pharisees saw him keeping this kind of company,
they had a fit, and lit into Jesus' followers. "What kind of example is this from your Teacher, acting cozy with crooks and riff-
raff?" Jesus, overhearing, shot back, "Who needs a doctor: the
healthy or the sick? Go figure out what this Scripture means: 'I'm
after mercy, not religion.' I'm here to invite outsiders,
not coddle insiders."*

Matthew 9:10 MSG

THE Church is not *your* church, but YOUR church is *the*
Church. Confused?

The Church is the past, present, and future collective of all
followers of Christ. It isn't a building or the people in the
building called your church. Your church is a department

within the larger "corporation" occupying a particular space and time. We are all responsible to each other, and we should appreciate the strengths of each and help overcome the weaknesses of each. The point is that you aren't alone. The group of people you might call a church is not an island, and you should have a global perspective of what the Church is because you are called into the greater community of believers—not just your local band of brothers.

The church's responsibility, much like a business organization directed by the CEO, is to equip and empower each individual to contribute to the successful accomplishment of its goals. The goals were designed to meet the vision around which the CEO built the company. God, our CEO, wants to be known, honored, and served through our loving him, which leads to loving others. That's the goal of the church—God, Inc.

There's a period of time early in your walk with Christ when you may be quite specific about how church should be done. You may even find it difficult to appreciate or even endure a service that doesn't meet the standards with which you have grown accustomed. I was just like that. I was once a pretty arrogant, young believer—and quite disrespectful. I once went as far as to chastise my first pastor, accusing him of not understanding adult non-Christians. It took many years of being exposed to many styles of worship and teaching to look past the presentation into the message, allowing God the room to be bigger than the quality of musicianship or choice of songs that week.

What I mean by allowing God to "be big" is to try not to limit your idea of his effectiveness by bringing his ability down to the same level of the weak attempts of man to express his love and power. God can do much with little if the hearts of those involved are sincere.

One night, I attended a service with a friend who was invited to a church unfamiliar to her. She received quite a shock when people coming forward for prayer started passing out left and right. My friend looked like she was torn between calling an ambulance or just beating a hasty retreat before anyone she knew found out we were there. Although she invited me to leave with her, I convinced her to stay. This was my first close-up encounter with a church where people were being "slain in the Spirit" as they call it. My friend was pretty freaked out. She didn't know quite what to do, but I found it a very important night for me.

Nope, I never felt led to walk forward or walk out, but that was actually the exciting part. I felt no pressure to be a part of a specific portion of the service, but I also did not feel apart from that body of believers. I actually easily focused on God and found myself worshiping without distraction. I didn't judge their form of worship, although I didn't understand it and didn't relate at all. In fact, I appreciated their desire to experience God and his desire to reach people wherever they are. I worshiped God that night in relationship with people I had nothing in common with but Christ. I now find myself in churches throughout the world, from ornate orthodox cathedrals to tiny two-room flats. The good news is that I now can find God there as well.

Have you been attending a church of some sort for a little while or a long time? Maybe you've felt an obligation to stay at your first church or the church of the friend who introduced you to Christ, but things aren't progressing the way you hoped. Maybe you think there might be something else out there and have a list of desires—things you wished were different about your church. What have you looked for already? What's on this list of yours?

"I want a place with people like me."

"I want to go somewhere with cool music, a building that doesn't look like a church, maybe one with dramas and kids programs."

"I want a church with a big singles group that does cool stuff."

"I want a pastor who's funny and can keep my interest."

These are certainly desires, things you want, but what do you need? Bottom line—you need a healthy church.

So, what is a healthy church? A friend of mine says, "The world is a hospital." Well, if that's true, then the church is Intensive Care. Churches should be full of broken people in need of healing. If a church is full of nothing but healthy-looking people and nobody seems to be confessing needs, sins, brokenness, fear, or doubt, then somebody's lying. That's a place full of secrets and closets full of pain. You will probably not find healing there.

I don't mean that church should be a weekly group counseling session; but a church should be a place where there is great grace for failure and also celebrations of freedom.

A church is a collection of different people, with unique issues, challenges, and backgrounds. Any given week the spiritual state of emotions and lives in a group, no matter how small, will radically vary. One thing is for certain, though, today a large part of your church, if you have one, is in need of prayer and support, and hopefully a bunch of others have great joy and celebrations to share. If the people of your church honestly express both sides of their life, the unfiltered good and bad, it's a healthy body where people grow close and bloom and connections stretch deep into the earth.

BOTTOM LINE

Right now what you need is a place to learn, admit need and ignorance, and receive help—a place that can help you get to know God. Nothing else really matters. Do whatever it takes to find a group of believers that you can learn from and even help by being their friend. It doesn't matter if they meet in a home, a beautiful church building or a burned out warehouse. All that matters is whether they are true to the Bible, try their best to honor God in all they do, and are a demonstration of God's grace and love as they grow you into a mature believer.

 TALK TO GOD:

Thank God for accepting you just as you are and ask him for the humility to accept others in their weakness. Also, ask for an opportunity to trust the Holy Spirit in another believer to give you the same grace that God gave you. Ask God to lead you to someone you can trust.

 DIG DEEPER:

Read Romans 15:1–13 again and note what you desire in a group of believers. If you have a group already, how can you play your part of acceptance and unity more? If you don't yet have a group of believers to grow with spiritually and relationally, pray for God's guiding hand and start looking for one.

Question 31

"What Church Is Perfect for Me?"

All the believers were one in heart and mind ... There were no
needy persons among them.

Acts 4:32, 34

Does the "perfect" church exist? Oh, sure, I have often attended the perfect church. Once, that "perfect" place was in complete and total disarray. Attendance was in decline, volunteerism was down, disagreements abounded, leaders were leaving, and it was in financial crisis. It was perfect precisely because of where I was in my relationship with God in that very context, and what I learned about God because I stayed. At that time, I was called to walk alongside seriously hurting people and I found blessings like few other times in my life. I discovered truth from God in amazingly deep ways while listening to the frustrations of others and helping them focus in the midst of crisis on who God is. It was the perfect chuch because I needed to hear God's truth in those circumstances and at that time as much as they did. I chose to allow God to give me compassion for others and acted on his leading instead of focusing on my own issues; I was encouraged daily, and grew in my knowledge of God instead of being brought down with the difficulties.

The church is made up of people, and we are far from perfect; but I emphatically believe there is a perfect place for you to attend. Perfect, though, must be qualified. Perfect does not mean a church that meets all of your needs. Perfect does not mean you agree with all the policies, leaders, messages, worship styles, or programs. Perfect means nothing more than that is the place where God desires you to be at that moment.

Surprisingly, during the time I mentioned above, I wasn't led to leave. Instead, I was led to catch the folks who fell out of the fold. The relationships that were built during the crisis in the church led to a Bible study in my home. The next step seemed natural.

After a few months, God introduced me to a group of people in another state investigating whether or not God was leading them to start a new church in my city. Soon thereafter, a new church was born. Several families relocated with the pastor to join my displaced group looking for a home and God's hand was shown in very validating ways. That church today is thriving with hundreds of members, and they even planted an additional church after only a few years.

There's no telling where that new church would be if I did not choose to stay in the midst of great turmoil with no good "logical" reason to remain. Sure, without me it could have just been delayed a year and that would have been no big deal. Regardless, what I do know is that I would have missed out completely on a greatly deepened understanding of God's care for his followers, seeing his power over our circumstances, and learning to trust that his plan is much grander than we could ever imagine.

My old church became very "wrong" for me in every way thinkable. Nothing about it appealed any longer to my style, or even to my personal desires for reaching people with spiritual questions and growing Christ followers. My favorite leaders and friends had already left, but I stayed because my emotions really had no bearing on whether it was the right place to be or not. When it was time to go, God made it quite plain; and what helped me see his leading was the choice to focus on what I could do to help wherever I saw need, not on my own issues.

The circumstances of whether a church is right or wrong for you cannot be answered simply. There may be many reasons to stay or go, but Christians commonly make one big mistake—they focus only on what the church can do for them, rather than what God can do in them by being there. If the purpose of living is to know God's character and love more every day, what exactly does that have to do with the style of worship or how engaging a speaker is? Sure, that can help connect you to God, but if those things are your only criteria for learning about and experiencing God, you are making the church instead of you responsible for that relationship. How much more should your relationships with believers impact your relationship with God, than anonymous attendance at a "professional" service?

A pastor at a very healthy church I attended stood up one Sunday and asked how many people were involved in weekly small group Bible studies. I think they called them "Care Groups" because the purpose was to do just that, always through the focus and leading of God. About 70 percent of that church raised their hands, which was amazing compared to most places I have been, but that wasn't good enough for him. He said that the goal of that church was 100 percent of its people in meaningful relationships with each other; so if you had to choose between attending the Sunday service or joining a small group study, skip Sunday.

Those were pretty bold words from a church leader, because there's no offering taken at a Bible study, no serving or volunteering for the attendees, and no tangible way to measure progress and success. Yet he knows that the purpose of the church is found in relationship, confession, and grace. That's the church visible: a body of believers growing in meaningful, God-honoring relationships with each other. If that body is focused on God's character, heart, and desires, its members will naturally be led into relationships with nonbelievers, serving the community, and serving each other. If they seek God collectively as well as individually, their desires will often align, and that's where great movements of God happen.

Smart Christians understand that anonymity is not what the Christian church is called to for a reason. As long as you stay at arm's length from other believers, your growth is dramatically stunted. If there isn't somebody at your church or Bible study who knows the story of your relationship with Christ, your struggles, and your hopes for the future, you better figure out if it is you or them who is holding back. Do all you can to build those relationships by first asking others those questions, and you will either find the perfect church for you in those relationships, or find you need to look elsewhere.

In addition to the value of relationships, a healthy church ensures that the Word of God, the Bible, is the center of all teaching. If you hear a message that is focused on counseling, good sounding words, and lots of fancy quotes but little or no biblical focus, you might want to keep your options open and continue to investigate. And make sure that you read the church's doctrinal statement. This is the description of the biblical truths they are guided by and will give you a baseline to determine if they are consistent with their teaching and God's Word.

BOTTOM LINE

Initially, you need a place where you can learn how to study the Bible and begin to understand the voice of God in everyday life. Once that foundation is built over your first couple of years, your options for worship and teaching style open up a great deal. You will have a better understanding of what is appropriate for you once you understand what God thinks. You need to learn to make good choices first and foremost, which means seeking wisdom from God—the source of all true wisdom. Find a place with people who will walk beside you down that path, and if they have goofy music and an ugly building, who cares?

TALK TO GOD:

Praise God for the unity he promises when believers focus on him. Ask him to guide you to the best way to contribute to the unity of the group of believers you are a part of or to guide you to the group of believers you need to join.

 DIG DEEPER:

Read Ephesians 3:14–21 and 4:1–16. What are Paul's desires for the attitude of the believers in the city of Ephesus? What about the actions of those people? What is not mentioned in these verses that is on your list of what you want in a church? If there are questions you have about your current group, write them down and find a leader to discuss them with.

Question 32

"Should I Give Money?"

*Each man should give what he has decided in his heart
to give, not reluctantly or under compulsion,
for God loves a cheerful giver.*

2 Corinthians 9:7

Big blonde hair, giant gold throne, multimillion dollar
homes, fancy cars, and soap opera tears dotting his $2000
designer suit—all that's missing is a gem-studded crown
atop that bleached white dome, but we see its reflection
nonetheless. This image of the money-hungry, cable TV evangelist is one of the reasons many people, myself included, not
only avoided Christianity for a time, but also still have problems sharing our finances even after Christ becomes a reality
to us.

When you first believe, there is a great deal to think about, wonder on, and investigate. Thinking about giving your money to a church while you are still figuring out what being a Christian is all about and who these people really are may be very far from the top of your list of priorities. For some, though, that is one of the first things they need to address.

What's right for you? What's wrong? Regardless of what anyone might tell you, what is right for you is not a set amount of money given at regular intervals. God is most interested in your heart, not your finances. But understand that he is relentless in acquiring your attention and devotion because he knows that is the only thing that grows, protects, and gives you joy. If money is in the way of your heart opening to God, if you are trusting more in money than his ability to provide for you, he might want you to deal with that issue very soon. If money isn't the biggest barrier in your life at the moment, if it is very easy for you to give, you just might need someone to help you discover what is right for you.

There are a few reasons why we give money as believers:

1. We don't consider it ours, anyway. Anything we have received is from God and should be considered a gift. If we worked for it, our abilities and opportunities were the gifts.

2. We want to contribute to the furthering of the work of God. Any time you help someone help others, such as by contributing to an organization or individual working with the needy locally or abroad, or providing for the church leaders serving you and your friends, you are serving. When you serve (giving of your time and energy) and give, you are growing to understand Christ's heart more deeply.

3. We want to trust God with every aspect of our lives. If your purpose in living is to know God's power and character and love more everyday, then he must sit in the place of honor

in every aspect of your life. Is he in charge of your financial situation or just an afterthought?

Does your heart shrink back and turn away at the thought of handing over your financial future to God? It has happened, at one time or another to everyone I know. You are in fine company. But the people who never pursued that uncomfortable feeling or allowed God to work on that part of their life never reached a clear conclusion about what to do with their money. They continuously face a bitterness and guilt that entraps them to some degree. On the other hand, those who pursued God's desires for their finances found peace and freedom in their souls, regardless of the weight of their wallets.

I cannot tell you what to give or when to give, but I can tell you why to give. You give what you choose to give because you desire to return to God what he has given you. If you do not think God has given you anything, you probably feel no need to give anything back. God desires our devotion more than our donations. If you aren't giving out of a desire to honor God, why are you giving? Is it so others will think highly of you and you hope it will help you better fit into the crowd? Or worse yet, is it out of guilt? If so, you are not only allowing people to control you, but you are also allowing a form of fear to rule your life. In that case, I would advise you to put your wallet back into your pocket and initiate a conversation with God on the topic. Look at what he says about giving (use a Bible with a concordance and look up "money" and "giving") and then look at your own emotions.

You have a lot to think about right now, and this may not be anything you need to deal with immediately. But if your heart stirs when the collection plate at church comes around, dig into that a bit and find out what's germinating.

The happiest financial moment of my life was not when I received the largest return I will likely ever receive on an investment but when I wrote the largest check I have ever written to give much of it away. For me, at that time, it was exactly where God wanted me to be. There was no stress, no fear about my future or my retirement, no calculating the loss of investment from compounded earnings over the next fifty years. Nope, there was just indescribable joy, and I was changed more by the knowledge of the impact of giving than the actual gift itself. That day changed my perspective on every dollar I've earned since.

God has a wonderful way of blessing us when we trust and give. Some folks will tell you that you will receive more money than you give, and I have known this to be true at times with many people. God does promise to bless our giving, but his definition of blessing might vary radically from our own.

What would you consider a greater gift: $100 or freedom from fear of money? What about $1000 or freedom from a fear of your future? What about a million dollars or greater understanding of God's power and love for you?

Who can put a price on peace?

BOTTOM LINE

When you act out of a desire in your spirit to honor God with your gifts instead of guilt or the compulsion of others, there are no regrets. Until then, keep your money. God wants your heart. God wants you to trust him. Eventually, everyone needs to address where they place their trust. When it's your day, you'll know. Right now, enjoy your God, and ask him where he wants to work next in your life. If you get a sense he wants you to address finances, ask how much, and feel free to seek counsel from others whom you trust.

TALK TO GOD:

Sit on a chair or couch in the room with the most stuff you own in it. Look around for five minutes without speaking, praying, or moving out of your seat. Think about all the stuff that you own or want to own. How much of your time in this present life is focused on owning things? Now think about the day you die and what difference the stuff you leave will make to people. What will have the most important lasting effect on people's lives? Thank God for all you have. Read Mark 12:41–44 and ask God to give you a heart such as that of the poor widow.

 ## DIG DEEPER:

Read Acts 4:32–5:11. Why did this happen to Ananias and his wife Sapphira? Why was God upset with them? Would this have happened if they gave nothing? Are you giving what you think you can or what you think God is leading you to give? Do you have a great desire to give, but don't know what to give? Try giving ten percent of your gross income, and give God an opportunity to provide for you and fill in the gaps. Inquire at your church or a Christian organization about their needs and how they remain accountable for the money they receive. Give with a joyful heart, but also be wise in your giving.

Question 33

"Why Pray Together?"

*Therefore encourage one another and build each other up,
just as in fact you are doing ... Be joyful always;
pray continually; give thanks in all circumstances,
for this is God's will for you in Christ Jesus.*

1 Thessalonians 5:11, 16–18

"I don't want to pray out loud; it makes me uncomfortable."

Have you ever heard this? Have you ever felt it?

I hear it all the time. There are people who love to pray in groups and people who just loathe the idea. I was the latter. For a time, like many people, I lived in anxiety whenever a group setting might call for me to pray. I kept hoping nobody would ask me to pray and reveal the terribly inexperienced, ignorant, stumbling words of the brand-new believer. It was just so hard to think about what I was to say in advance of saying it, and sometimes my words fell out incoherently. I just didn't sound as eloquent as the pastor or those people who grew up praying; it made me feel stupid, so what was the point.

That's a good question. What's the point of prayer, anyway? Whether conducted in groups or alone, at its core prayer should be about God. We pray to honor God; to know his heart and desires for us; to present our requests because we think it matters; to ask forgiveness; to grow in trust; to praise him and to remind ourselves of his attributes like goodness, love, power, and mercy. Prayer is about God first and foremost, and not about us, if it is to be anything good and beneficial.

In prayer, if we allow it, God's Spirit is at work in us, guiding us to his desires—interceding, translating, influencing. As the truth of God is revealed in prayer, we are changed. Prayer can change us only because of this connection through his Spirit, whether we feel it or not.

God even says that when we don't know what to pray for, the Spirit intercedes on our behalf and prays for us in ways beyond our comprehension. So we don't have to worry about doing it "right" ourselves. God knows what's on our hearts because his Spirit is hangin' out in there, rooting around in all the little spaces, looking for reality even when we don't know what is real. If God knows what we need even when we don't, then God knows what the person next to you needs, even if you don't.

How would you feel if a close friend said, "Hey, I have been invited to speak in front of the President of the United States, the Pope, the United Nations, fifty country leaders, the one-hundred richest people, and the world's most famous actors and musicians, all in personal meetings that will be broadcast to the whole world on TV and the Internet. I want to tell them about you and your needs. I want to make an impassioned plea for whatever you want me to ask on your behalf"?

If you were really shy, that might freak you out. If you were in need, however, that would be a wonderful gift. You would probably receive a lot of stuff from people whose hearts were touched. Certainly, the odds are in your favor of somebody giving up something, and you would probably end up with more than you needed. But the most touching aspect would be that your friend loved you so much as to be your representative to that most crucial audience.

There is something amazing that happens in your soul when someone prays for you. The very idea that someone would choose to intercede with the Creator of the Universe on your behalf is a pretty cool thing. He placed the sun in the heavens, knows the name of every star in every galaxy, and he will keep the earth spinning until the end of time. What could be more valuable than having someone willingly (and often joyfully) approach the throne of God and speaking for you?

Isn't that a gift you'd like to give others? Are you really willing to let the fear of shame or embarrassment keep you from offering that gift to others? What does that say about your attitude toward the hearts of the very friends who talk to God for you? Are they really that judgmental? Would they laugh? If so, why on earth are you spending any time whatsoever with them? Get new friends!

I'm guessing that they really aren't that bad—they probably even have the Spirit of God working in them. So why not take the chance and talk to God on their behalf? God will certainly not be keeping score of your "ability to pray well." It was God who chose tongue-tied Moses to speak to the most important ruler on the planet, Pharaoh, on behalf of his people. Moses begged to be let off the hook but instead God gave him the power of his Spirit.

When it comes down to it, I have never found a logical reason for not praying together. In reality, your fears are robbing you of the possibility of experiencing the power of God for yourself. Your insecurities are robbing you of the joy of giving an amazing gift to someone else. You will never know how much you (or they) are missing until you try it for yourself.

Praying together also has the added benefit of knitting your souls together. Praying together shows you love each other and will actually help you love each other more. Because you choose to pray together, you will grow in greater understanding and love of God. How? As his Spirit promises to guide the prayers of those who desire that leading, the stuff that comes out of peoples' mouths becomes a mosaic of truth and together makes a remarkable masterpiece. If God can work in an individual, think of what he can create from the prayers of a dedicated group.

So, what can we expect when we pray together?

God influences and inspires

Prayer partners are prompted to think about something in a new way or think on something completely new that then guides their prayers.

God speaks

If God wants to tell someone something very clearly, he may choose to communicate through the voice of another.

God reveals himself

You are reminded of attributes of God that you may have forgotten, or you may discover something new about him.

God convicts

Through the words of the confession of others and your own silence as you listen, the Holy Spirit has room to work in your heart in ways he cannot when you are speaking.

God forgives

Genuine confession to God always leads to grace. Confession to God in a group adds a hug.

The most inspiring, heartfelt moments of prayer I have ever experienced have been the prayers of a child, the words of the new believer, and the grace-filled stumbles of a genuine heart with untrained speech. God asks us to come to him like little children—in honesty and sincerity, not with the polished words of an orator. All he wants is our hearts, confessed as best we can through our words. He wants this alone, and he wants to use this to encourage others.

BOTTOM LINE

If you are afraid to pray with others, you are robbing yourself and them of a wonderful gift of grace and truth. You are limiting the opportunities for the Holy Spirit to speak, for you to be changed, and for some of those last locked prison doors of fear to be opened. This isn't about doing anything right; this is about faith that God loves you and his love is manifest in those who follow him. If you trust God, you must learn to trust others who feel the same way and live as such.

TALK TO GOD:

Read Romans 8:26–27. Ask God's Spirit to guide your prayers. Ask him to help your words bless someone else.

DIG DEEPER:

Step #1: Start small. Pray one sentence—the thing you want to say, but are afraid to say—the next time you are in group prayer.

Step #2: The next time a fellow believer shares a need, ask if you can stop and pray for him or her. Do it then. Try putting your hand on his or her shoulder to help make a tangible connection in your mind that you are speaking to God for a real person. Try closing your eyes to help you clear your head. Be quiet for a moment and ask God's Spirit to guide you. They won't think you are weird. Then simply speak what comes out and say "Amen" when you have no other thoughts running around in your head.

Question 34

"I'm No Evangelist, Am I?"

*Commit to the LORD whatever you do, and your
plans will succeed.*

Proverbs 16:3

*Fear of man will prove to be a snare, but whoever trusts
in the LORD is kept safe.*

Proverbs 29:25

After a quiet, momentary pause, the darkness is broken as
the house lights come up. With a cue from the emcee's eyes,
every head turns to see the star of the movie walk to the
front of the screen. He eases down onto a stool, briefly
acknowledging the applause of the crowd as if he's heard it
one too many times this week. He's not ungrateful, just

weary from travel. It's another movie premiere, and although this one is in Phoenix, Arizona, I've grown accustomed to the program after living for over five years in Utah (home of the Sundance Film Festival). It's time for the Q&A, and I assume I'll sit and fidget, as usual, hoping it ends quickly. This time, though, God has an unexpected lesson in store for me.

The actor is Kevin Spacey and the movie, although it is immaterial to this story, is *The Life of David Gale*. The significant impact on my life comes from witnessing the answer to a simple question asked by a teenage girl desiring to become a professional actress. This shy young girl on the front row sheepishly raised her hand and posed this question to the successful actor:

"Have you ever been nervous at an audition? If so, how did you get over that?"

Kevin stood up and pulled his lips together and back in that simple, gentle way that reveals a heart of compassion and empathy. With his eyes softened and his head cocked ever so slightly to one side, he revealed that he knew what she was going through, and he wanted to help—first her nervousness, second her question. He walked over to her, stood just two feet from her chair, and pulled her into a private room of conversation.

Her name was Jennifer, as I recall, and after assessing her fears with a few simple questions, he changed her whole perspective.

"Jennifer, when you're standing there in front of strangers you must see the world from their eyes. You must remember that they want you to succeed. You see, these folks have a problem and they are hoping you are the solution. They're in your corner, no matter how it appears. They want you to do well."

Do you and Jennifer have something in common? Do you think of God in the way that Jennifer thought of casting directors?

"God only sees my flaws and mistakes."

"I'm probably not good enough to be chosen for a significant part."

"I'm sure I'm not even the type he wants."

"If I don't get it exactly right, he'll pick someone else, but I'm not even sure what he's looking for. How on earth can I do a good job?"

I want to redirect the advice Kevin Spacey shared with that young aspiring actress. I want to help you develop a proper perspective concerning God. You see, God has a problem he wants you to help him solve. It's a problem of sin, brokenness, and loneliness. It's the problem of separation that has existed between God and mankind since the Garden of Eden. And God wants you to help solve that problem.

Imagine that you're the only one asked to apply for the part. God knew all along that you were perfect for this role. No audition is necessary. The role was written with you in mind. You were typecast, and the only thing required of you is to accept the part and show up. Will you accept the part designed perfectly for you?

If so, when you perform under the direction of God, people's hearts will be moved and their lives changed. It's hard to see while it's going on, but the end result is remarkable. During the filming of movies like *The Lord of the Rings* and *The Matrix*—the greatest special effects films of their time— the actors often spoke of how difficult it was to picture the end product while they were filming. They acted in front of blank blue screens, fighting non-existent foes, riding among a handful of horses but pretending they were a part of a mighty army of thousands. The director had a vision and a large role in making all the components work together. The actors played a part, but simply had to trust in that vision while giving it their all.

That's what your whole life is like, but it is most evident when sharing your faith. You may not be sure what the final product will look like, but you can be assured that the vision of the director is perfect, and the role you're selected to play is perfect for you. Also, you should understand that this director is involved before, during, and after you perform your lines and action scenes. What isn't perfect in front of the camera can be cleaned up in the editing room, with special effects, or additional scenes. The director alone takes responsibility for the final outcome of this story—the story of grace in each individual's life. So why not relax and enjoy being a part of it.

BOTTOM LINE

Trust in the director and play your part. The movie is bigger than you and no scene rests solely on the shoulders of one actor. Enjoy yourself and be amazed that the final product is incredibly grander than you could have ever imagined beforehand.

Talk to God:

Think about the people who were involved in your process of discovering the life-changing truth of Jesus. Praise God for bringing them into your life. Ask that God continues to bless them.

 ## Dig Deeper:

Make a list of the people you prayed about and write down the importance they had in your spiritual life. Call, e-mail, or meet face to face to tell them what their time and caring meant to you. Then ask how their involvement in your getting to know Christ has impacted their understanding of and relationship with God. You will be amazed at how much God blessed them through helping you.

Question 35

"How Do I Explain the Changes in Me?"

But in your hearts set apart Christ as Lord. Always be prepared to give an answer to everyone who asks you to give the reason for the hope that you have. But do this with gentleness and respect.

1 Peter 3:15

Hey, Mom, what's been going on with Michael? In the last ten months, he has really changed."

One month after Christ became a reality to me, I heard that people close to me had noticed changes in my character and attitude beginning nine months before I ever made that decision. My sister had no idea I was going to church, investigating the existence of God, and pursuing truth in the Bible and Jesus—but long before anything "officially" happened in my soul, the journey to salvation left a remarkable imprint. I, unfortunately, was completely oblivious.

At the time my mother told me about this conversation with my sister, I was wondering if anything was actually different at all. With a few old sins rearing their ugly heads and quickly creating doubt, my faith had staggered to one knee. But hearing that evidence existed outside my perspective, standing in my faith became easier.

People will notice what you don't. They will ask. Don't be surprised, even if you don't see what they see. You must be prepared to answer.

A young university student in Russia, where cheating on tests is often attributed to the lax attention of many professors, was faced with a great dilemma as a new believer. She could continue to cheat or trust that her faith and hard work would be enough. So, on her next test she chose not to use the cheat sheet notes she normally brought to class. She passed, albeit with a lower grade.

Her friends noticed and were amazed. Not so much at her passing without cheating, but in wonderment that she would ever want to. Everybody cheated. It was just done. Why buck the system? They kept curious watch as she passed another test, but her grade point average dropped again.

She prepared for their questions in advance with her spiritual mentor and was ready when they asked. She spoke of the joy she found in the honest path, and how she discovered that her identity wasn't wrapped up in being like everybody else. She shared how she actually experienced a greater freedom without the guilt and fear of cheating. The fact that she didn't care if they thought her odd was quite intriguing to them. Where did this newfound confidence come from? Why didn't she care to be like everybody else? Can you actually live without succumbing to peer pressure?

Four girls decided that this honest path was worth a try, and now an entire group of students at different stages of belief in God are trying to live by biblical principles. They are changing as they walk down this path to truth in Jesus because someone was willing to answer with confidence why she had changed.

There is no need to make this explanation of change into a religious discussion or bop people over the head with a Bible. Tell them the truth in plain English, and if they ask the "why" and "what led you to this decision" questions, then feel free to mention that there are recent changes to your spiritual perspective that are impacting the way you live. If they are not interested in spiritual things yet, they'll step out of that conversation gracefully. If they ask more, they are giving you permission to tell them your story.

BOTTOM LINE

You have a new identity and others see it even if you don't. Many people are thinking questions, even if they aren't saying them out loud yet. That time will come. Assess how you are living and thinking differently, maybe by asking people you know, and be prepared to respond to inquiries. Seek guidance from a spiritual mentor and pray for God's Spirit to guide your response. Trust God, speak truth, respect the person, and you will discover in the telling of your story the joy of God's passion that can be experienced in no other way.

TALK TO GOD:

Thank God for the changes in you and for promising to complete this work. Ask him to reveal how he is molding you and making you more like Christ.

 ## DIG DEEPER:

What do you hope for? What do you really believe about your future because of God's miraculous influence and perfect character? Do you believe that your marriage, whether present or future, will last? Do you believe that you will not fear death when it is your time? Do you believe that you will never receive more pain in your life than you can bear? Write these hopes down, and maybe even pin them up somewhere you can see them or slip them into your journal to read on occasion. After that, dig into why you hope for these things. What about your experience and knowledge of God led to this hope? This is one of the most important things you can ever do as a believer. This little exercise can change your entire life if you really take the time to think and pray it through.

Question 36

"How Do I Get All My Friends and Family to Trust in Christ?"

≈

Here is a trustworthy saying that deserves full acceptance: Christ Jesus came into the world to save sinners—of whom I am the worst. But for that very reason I was shown mercy so that in me, the worst of sinners, Christ Jesus might display his unlimited patience as an example for those who would believe on him and receive eternal life. Now to the King eternal, immortal, invisible, the only God, be honor and glory forever and ever. Amen.

1 Timothy 1:15–17

"He did what? No way! Is he in some kind of cult? Was it a nervous breakdown? He seemed so normal before. I had no idea he was capable of something like this."

I remember that day very well. One of the regional directors of the company I worked for announced to the entire eastern region that he was "born again" and had become an "entirely new man" in an instant. He turned in his resignation, and soon left his job to do ... well, we had no idea what. He was on the way out and figured he had nothing to lose, so during his last couple of weeks he made a point to meet with every individual on his staff one by one to talk to them about Jesus Christ, share his story, and ask them to make the same decision he had.

There were no takers. Not that there couldn't have been, but his approach assumed too much. He failed to understand why everyone wasn't as excited about his decision as he was. He also failed to understand that the only change in him that was evident was that he suddenly became kind of freaky and weird. He was deemed one to be avoided at all costs rather than one to be sought out for guidance. We didn't know if he really wanted to stop sleeping around on his wife or lying about his sales numbers or drinking with the boys late into the night. Frankly, we had no reason to believe any of it. We had a right to be skeptical.

I knew what he was going through because I had accepted Christ just a few months earlier. The change I felt within me was so real that I couldn't imagine others didn't identify it straight away. They saw something, but didn't know what it was. They presumed that I was still the rude, selfish guy that just seemed to be having a good day. I wanted everyone to know, but usually when I would approach the subject with someone they clammed up. Sometimes they listened;

sometimes they made it clear I was intruding. I quickly broke relationship with several people through my enthusiasm, thrashing about like an over-caffeinated, far-sighted bull in a china shop.

Then as I was asking God for help (as a last resort, mind you), he chose to lead me to the verse about responding to answers and made it very clear that my approach was wrong. GOD was responsible for their salvation, not me. He invited me to be involved for the purpose of knowing him more. I then chose to live my life seeking God, and let the consistency of the change in me convince people that I truly had changed. It worked and allowed me to be more purposeful in entering the lives of others without being rude. Once people believed I was different, they asked why. Until then, my actions meant much more than words.

Now when they asked, I was able to tell them about the hope I had for the future, how I found peace, how my anxiousness about performance and success was beginning to melt away. Once the people were convinced I was different and trusted that I would speak to them in love and not judgment, they wanted to hear my story.

BOTTOM LINE

You've been given the most awesome gift and you naturally want to share it with those you love. Do you believe he loves them more than you do? Can you trust God to save the people you care about? Ask him to involve you in that process. Wait for God. Ask for guidance. Enter their lives to love them and be ready to answer when they ask why.

TALK TO GOD:

Ask God for sensitivity to the spiritual journey of the people you care for and also for sensitivity to the leading of the Holy Spirit. Ask how you can show them Christ's love without saying a word about Jesus, but remain open to words if prompted. Pray for the unsaved people in your life—that they would be open to the wooing of the Holy Spirit.

 ## DIG DEEPER:

Study 1 Timothy 1:15–17. Your first time reading it through, note on a piece of paper every word or phrase that represents an action or desire of Jesus Christ. The second time reading, note attributes of Jesus/God. On your third time through, pay special attention to the role of Paul (the author). What happened to him? What was he like before? Now, given all of this "data," how did Paul expect these truths to be communicated through his life to nonbelievers? How can they be communicated through your life?

Question 37

"Why Do I Need to Tell People about Jesus?"

Then Jesus came to them and said, "All authority in heaven and on earth has been given to me. Therefore go and make disciples of all nations, baptizing them in the name of the Father and of the Son and of the Holy Spirit, and teaching them to obey everything I have commanded you. And surely I am with you always, to the very end of the age."

Matthew 28:18–20

"Why do I need to tell people about Jesus?"

"I'm not qualified; I know so little about the Bible."

"Why do I have to be involved; can't they just go to church and talk to a pastor?"

"I'm not a pastor or an evangelist. I can't answer anyone's questions; I'm still trying to figure it out myself."

Do these thoughts sound familiar? Have you had these same thoughts or ones like them? It is extremely common and normal to think this way because of how evangelism is looked at in the world. The whole idea of sharing your faith has been tainted by rude people who interrupt and argue with total strangers, who have little regard for the current journey of the individual. Sharing your faith isn't about having all the answers, doing things a certain way, or training. It is about being amazed at God, understanding his heart in a way that connects you with his greatest passion for mankind, and being obedient to the leading of his Spirit in daily life. The "how" and "why" of talking to people about your beliefs is covered at length in another book of mine entitled *Permission Evangelism – When to Talk, When to Walk*, but I want you to understand a bit of the "why" now.

Forcing someone to the end of the journey before they are ready is akin to picking up a backpacker in your car and driving him to the end of the trail, then asking him to describe the joy of the hiking journey to someone else. Was his experience real and valuable without him walking the path in his own way, in his own time? The journey is certainly about the destination, but without experiencing the path to that point, the destination loses a great deal of its value. Regardless of why someone may choose to get in the car and skip the self-driven footpath, if he intends and needs to actually understand the value of the path all along, he will eventually need to walk it on his own.

I have found that the people who were allowed the time to come to their own conclusions without pressure, but who were guided along the path, entered into a deeper, more mature faith considerably faster than those who jumped to an emotional or coerced decision. Therefore, sharing your faith is about sharing your journey and asking to be involved in someone else's. That's how you relate to anyone regardless of socioeconomic status, age, or geography.

The "therefore" in the verse from Matthew 28 is possible because God is in control. You can go talk to people about him and his Spirit will be with you always to guide and teach you. Sharing your faith is about God, not you. It is about him being glorified and both people involved in the conversation discovering more about him. So if you feel unprepared, you are in the perfect place. You just need to get your motives in line with God's desires for you.

Everything involved in talking to people about Jesus is about relationship—yours with them, and both of yours with God. Frankly, I share my faith for selfish reasons. I want to know God. I want to feel what God feels, see what he sees, hear what he hears, and know what he knows, at whatever degree is available to me on this earth. That is like the intimate relationship between a husband and wife. That's pretty intimate.

I can't explain it any better than I already have in *Permission Evangelism*, so here is an excerpt about learning of God's character by sharing your faith. I have included some of that text below:

> None of us will ever fully fathom God, and I would not even venture to try in this book, but I must take a shot at the aspects of God's character that are revealed through evangelism. God is love—it is his love for all his creation that compels his desire for the lost and

his mercy that made restoration possible. It is his love and goodness that invites us to participate in evangelism for the benefits it brings to the believer. God is holy and just—worthy of our honor. As we draw closer to him through evangelism, we see that he alone is worthy of our worship.

The quest for understanding God's heart is your responsibility. There is nothing else more important in life than knowing God, which should naturally result in glorifying him. It was the purpose mankind was created for, but as Christians, we spend most of our lives and prayers focused on learning about God in context of his relationship with us. We earnestly seek God's heart to change us, but I believe we don't always begin our search in the right place. Our desire to please God is more often focused on our sin and how we can change to be more like Christ. We will always fall short of our own expectations to be Christ-like if our growth in relationship with God is focused on ourselves.

If our heart's desire is to please God, we should focus on where God finds his greatest joy—and that is NOT the church. As difficult as it may be to accept, God loves you dearly, but you are not his greatest passion. In the parable of the lost lamb (Luke 15:3–7), Jesus teaches that heaven's greatest joy is in the safe return of the one lost lamb to the fold, NOT in the ninety-nine who don't need saving. We don't like to think of God's joy in these terms because our own selfishness desires us to be the only object of God's love. Since our salvation we are now one with Christ in heart and purpose. We are therefore, one in passion—if we allow the connection by relinquishing our selfish desire to be the only child.

God's desire is for intimate relationship with humanity—we like to think of this as a great mystery, but God has chosen to reveal it to us. God didn't create man because he needs us. Being complete in the Trinity, he chose to create us anyway because love, the essence of God, glorifies and honors the giver. Our purpose is not found in merely "being," but being in loving relationship with our Creator. True life—spiritual, purposeful, and joyful—is found only in relationship with God and his family.

WHAT'S IN IT FOR US?

Have you ever been around someone who is in the midst of one of life's joy-filled moments—getting engaged, having a baby, achieving a lifetime goal. Joy is infectious—you want to be with them, hear the story again, participate in the moment because it makes you feel good, too. Even if the person is a stranger to you, it feels good to see someone so happy. Now imagine that the individual is someone close to you—someone you love, someone you want to please. What does seeing and feeling their joy do for you? What is God's greatest joy? God's greatest joy is being reconnected with sinners. It is the reason why God endured his greatest pain, Christ on the cross. His desire is never quenched. He seeks the repentance of sinners above all else. If God's greatest joy is when a lost soul finds him, don't you want to be there? Doesn't it make sense to be involved in God's greatest joy?

God's character—love, goodness, faithfulness—requires that all his actions toward us be for our benefit. There's always something in it for us. God does nothing halfway, so when we are in the service of God, we are blessed. Our participation in the process of bringing the unsaved to him is not for his benefit or for the benefit of the lost. We should evangelize for us! Sounds selfish only if you don't consider that God loves us and desires to bless us in everything we do."[5]

BOTTOM LINE

There is no way you can understand God in the way he desires without sharing in his greatest passion. If you maintain a vertical-only relationship (that is, a relationship between you and God, but not between you and others), your joy will be limited and your life will not shine as God intended. BUT, if you do step out to be involved in the thing you cannot do without God, you will understand his heart, his sadness, and his amazing joyfulness in remarkable ways. You will grow in faith because you will know it was not you, but rather God through you, that accomplished anything in someone else's spiritual life. And you will be inspired to drink deep of his words and take responsibility for your faith.

Again, the question you must ask is not "Why?" but "Why not?" If the answer is about you and fear, great—you just found out why God wants you to take this step.

Talk to God:

What do you think and feel about God's passion to pursue relationship with you? Talk to him about that. Ask for his passion to grow in you so that you can understand his heart.

 # Dig Deeper:

Make a list of all the reasons you don't want to tell someone about Jesus. Next to each line item, write down if God is capable of overcoming it. After that, write down how you can enable him the opportunity to demonstrate that power.

Question 38

"How Do I Deal with Rejection?"

≋

Everyone who wants to live a godly life in
Christ Jesus will be persecuted

2 Timothy 3:12

"You aren't my friend if you don't _____!"

"If you mention God one more time, you're gonna be out on the street."

"Oh, come on, don't be so boring. You used to love doing that."

"Don't bring that holy roller, Christian nonsense in here."

"If you pray or talk about God here anymore, you'll be fired."

"I thought you were normal. I used to like you. I didn't know you were one of them."

Somebody hates you. I mean, he hates everything about you. He detests being in your presence. Just being near you makes him feel sick.

His name is Satan.

But that seems okay because he's bad, and you can't even see him. It's a good sign that he hates you because it means God is alive in you, and Satan really hates God. It's God he rejects, but it would be perfectly fine if it was just you he hated, right? I mean, who wants to be Satan's friend, anyway?

On the other hand, other people—maybe some of your best friends or close family—have started avoiding you, stopped calling, and maybe they even act rude and condescending when you're together. That really hurts. Those are people you care about and with whom you desire healthy relationships. It seems they are forcing you to choose between living the way God says you should live now and the way they live.

If this hasn't happened yet, it will. Sorry to bring what seems like bad news, but it is a biblical fact of life.

Sometimes it isn't so clear-cut that others are rejecting you because they reject your choices. It often is unspoken, but painfully obvious. Why are they suddenly giving you the cold shoulder when you don't really feel like you are doing anything all that different than before? Why do the guys at the office stop cussing around you or cut off the dirty joke before the punch line when you walk up?

It's because they see something in you that you don't. It's because their spirit is in conflict with yours. It's him again—the guy who hates you, that Satan guy—but manifest in the unspoken and probably unknown fear of God in others. You can't really see it, actually, because it is just who you are now. It is your essence, your new reality, your spirit, a new being in the same skin—it is God in you they are rejecting.

Sin is dark, but sometimes sin feels safe because sin is a known entity when you're accustomed to living in darkness. When the light of God's Spirit enters the same room as sin, sin scurries away and hides in a corner for fear of being destroyed. Light exposes lies and reveals truth, but truth is often painful and scary. Truth revealed always requires change. Some will be drawn to the light like a flower to the sun, and some will scurry like a cockroach in the kitchen when surprised in the night.

There is a light in you that is Christ's Spirit. Regardless of the intensity, light always changes its environment unless it is covered up and hidden. Focused and concentrated, light can cut through steel, remove a tumor, or entertain the masses with beautiful pictures in the sky. A simple candle can reveal reality, clear a path, remove fear, or expose danger. Light is life to plants, people, and animals that were made for it and death for many creatures of the earth living in dark places.

Because you are a visual representation of God's Spirit, those who are convicted by truth will reject you. You will face choices to follow the crowd and continue sinning or to stand firm in the freedom found in obedience to God. Other people's responses to your choices will reveal their issues with trusting God. Your response to the need for their acceptance is your issue with trusting God. Therefore, if you are in relationship with people who do not know God, and you live as though you do, then you will be faced with crossroads of moral decision over and over and over.

You will not fit in.

BUT, because of this you can be the light that shows the path to their freedom—the path to Jesus. You can be the key that unlocks the prison of peer pressure, fear of rejection, and known sins that trap, maim, and destroy. You can be a beacon of hope to the lost if you allow that light to shine through your words that build up instead of destroy, your silence that refuses to lash out when attacked, and your confidence to do the right thing when nobody else has the guts or desire.

If you stand firm, and live by the truth you profess of God's power, love, and character, many of those very ones who attack and reject you will eventually turn to you for freedom.

BOTTOM LINE

Whether or not you will be rejected is not even a question. How you will respond to that rejection is something you must purposefully decide in advance. If not, you will forever flail about, hoping bad things won't happen, and avoiding the obedience to the truth that defines the quality of your relationship with God. What are you afraid of, really? You can either fear man or fear God—your choice simply defines whom you desire to please. If you choose truth over comfort, your response is clear and the only true comfort can then be found. What price truth? Ask God to draw the lines, and make a decision to stand firm. You won't be alone. There's a light that will keep you warm and safe.

TALK TO GOD:

Thank God for never compromising to accomplish his objectives to bring you to a greater knowledge of him. Ask him for the wisdom and strength to be uncompromising in your own purity regardless of the consequences. Ask God to help you develop a healthy fear of him, by understanding more of his power and love. Tell him if that is a scary prayer. Ask him to reveal anything that is in the way of your desire for holiness.

 # DIG DEEPER:

Make a list of relationships that you are unwilling to put at risk for the sake of your relationship with God and your beliefs. Which ones really make your heart hurt to think about losing? God may not ask you to lose those relationships, but he wants you to prioritize your relationship with him over anyone else. Is there a relationship you value more than Jesus? Ask God to grow your love for him so that it exceeds your love for anyone else. Only then can you perfectly love them in a balanced relationship.

Question 39

"Why Am I Called to Serve Others?"

You, my brothers, were called to be free. But do not use your free-
dom to indulge the sinful nature; rather, serve one
another in love.

Galatians 5:13

Man, was I ashamed of myself. After meeting a very normal seventeen-year-old high school student and his girlfriend and learning about their regular visits to a retirement home to give pedicures to elderly women, I was momentarily grossed out. Handling any stranger's feet—not just an old, wrinkly, stranger's feet—would make me wince a little.

After hearing of their joy in entering the life of these often forgotten people to give them what they least expected, but most needed—love, dignity, and the chance to feel beautiful again—I desired to join in. Their experience of serving influenced my desires, and so it is over and over and over. Imagine what can happen when a big group of people shares their stories of frowns erased, thirsts quenched, and loneliness pushed to a distant memory. Serving and sacrifice—what you give—introduces you to Christ's heart more than anything you can receive from others.

Direct personal development through study and prayer will only take you so far in your journey toward spiritual maturity. Service to others—in a church or Christian organization or on your own—can facilitate a deeper understanding of humility and its value. Humility is much about considering others' needs more than your own, which then leads you to focus less on yourself. Helping others, especially in areas that might be uncomfortable for you, leads you to rely on God, learn of his power, and drink deeply of his caring heart for all mankind.

Serving can begin in the simplest of ways, such as by spending time with someone and just listening to him. If you stay quiet long enough and seek God for direction, where or how you can serve them will surely become evident. Your church has needs and few volunteers to fill those needs, so I can guarantee you'll find unlimited opportunities there. I do recommend, though, that you seek out its needs and not just what you want to do. If it is effective at volunteerism, the organization will assess your spiritual gifts and attempt to place you somewhere that can best leverage who God created you to be. But be open to the possibility that God wants to teach you something about your character no matter what you choose. I can't tell you what to do, but I can tell you where you should end up.

Ultimately, as you grow in spiritual maturity, you should be actively helping others grow in their relationships with God through teaching, serving, funding, or through whatever gift God has given to you. As you purposefully enter into relationship with people, learning of their needs, serving should become quite natural. It doesn't have to look like leading a Bible study or preaching at a church, but as you grow in wisdom and knowledge of God you will have people come to you for guidance, direction, and help of all sorts. Pointing them to Christ and helping them grow in that relationship will assist their maturing as a person—and yours.

The process of growing in maturity gets to the point where it stops being just about you and God and starts being about other people as well. There's a balance to knowing God, and identifying the needs of others is part of that. God sees their needs as well as yours, and he will lead you into the relationship opportunities for serving and giving that will both help others discover more of God and enhance your experience.

It all begins with taking one tiny step into whatever opportunity, however small, God presents to serve someone else. That's where joy is often found—doing the thing you never thought was possible and knowing it wasn't accomplished alone. Every time I allow God to accomplish the seemingly impossible through me, my mind immediately dreams of new possibilities. If it's God doing it, is anything impossible? What a way to live!

BOTTOM LINE

Giving and serving others always stretches us if God is in it because he desires that you learn more of him in the process. If giving and serving is easy, comfortable, and never challenging, are you doing it solely in your own power and not trusting

God with that part of your life? Faith is always about trusting in something outside of your ability to control. Always look at your service and giving through this filter. Go ahead, step into the uncomfortable and do something for someone other than yourself—and in so doing, do the most wonderful thing for yourself that you can do—grow in faith.

 TALK TO GOD:

This is a great time to talk to God about understanding Jesus' heart for you. Thank him for being brutalized, taunted, shamed, and murdered for you, even though you rejected him for so long. Ask him for change in your heart so you can know compassion and love that would create a desire to serve others with his Spirit regardless of their response

 DIG DEEPER:

Read Ephesians 6:7–8. Who do you serve by virtue of their position in your work, school, or volunteering? Does the word "serve" make you uncomfortable? Do you act as Paul instructs in this verse? How can you serve someone in authority in a way that shows the love of Christ? Read Galatians 5:22–23 and assess what fruits you display to the people in authority over you. Now, think about who you can serve that is not above you in authority, but may be technically a peer or below you. Pray for an opportunity to serve them, and see if your attitude toward them changes.

Question 40

"Do I Really Understand This Christian Life?"

*Now when he saw the crowds, he went up on a mountainside
and sat down. His disciples came to him, and he began to
teach them, saying:*

> *"Blessed are the poor in spirit,
> for theirs is the kingdom of heaven.*
>
> *Blessed are those who mourn,
> for they will be comforted.*
>
> *Blessed are the meek,
> for they will inherit the earth.*
>
> *Blessed are those who hunger and thirst for righteousness,
> for they will be filled.*
>
> *Blessed are the merciful,
> for they will be shown mercy.*
>
> *Blessed are the pure in heart,
> for they will see God.*
>
> *Blessed are the peacemakers,
> for they will be called sons of God.*

*Blessed are those who are persecuted because of righteousness,
for theirs is the kingdom of heaven."*

Matthew 5:1–10

When we become Christians, our lives change because our hearts are brand-new. I see in these words the life of Christ, certainly, and an amazing ideal of which we get glimpses as we enable the Holy Spirit to rule in our hearts. But there's also something deeper, more profound: a path, if you will, outlining the steps to that very life.

Look at the sections above individually and then see them together as a chronological progression, each following and building upon the other.

"Blessed are the poor in spirit"

Before you came to Christ, you first realized that you had a sinful heart and were powerless to overcome it. Your spirit was not up to snuff compared to God's holiness. Your actions came from your core nature, a sinful nature, that you were powerless to overcome.

"Blessed are those who mourn"

What do you mourn? Well, death, of course. "For the wages of sin is death, but the gift of God is eternal life in Christ Jesus our Lord" (Rom. 6:23). After you realized your sin, you lamented the resulting despair in life and separation from God.

"Blessed are the meek"

When you reach this point and you are hit with the realization of your utter helplessness to make things right, you are humbled and accept your need for help.

"Blessed are those who hunger and thirst for righteousness"

Some people just accept this reality as life and try to mask their despair at this stage. Maybe you did, too, but eventually you stopped fighting and desired change. You desired a new heart, a new life, and a new future. You desired truth. You desired to know God. You confessed your sin, asked for forgiveness, and accepted Christ's sacrifice on your behalf.

"Blessed are the merciful"

You are shown mercy and now can be merciful to others. For the first time in your life you have been forgiven, cleansed, and have received what you most needed, when you least deserved it. You received grace. Now, for the first time, you understand what real forgiveness and mercy is all about.

"Blessed are the pure in heart"

You are now a new creation in Christ Jesus. The old is gone and the new is born (2 Cor. 5:17). With this new nature you are capable of acting out of a pure heart. What once seemingly fit perfectly into your life, into your heart, now seems foreign. You receive conviction and guilt for things that once gave you pleasure, however temporary. Your desires and responses begin to change.

"Blessed are the peacemakers"

You now can live life as an ambassador of reconciliation (2 Cor. 5:20). You have the power to unite people through love instead of destroying through selfishness and pride. You can love your enemies, and be obedient to authority once you trust that God is in charge, and works all things for good (Rom. 8:28). You influence others to reconcile with God and make their own peace, a peace you can now explain using your own story.

"Blessed are those who are persecuted because of right-eousness"

You are now different from the world around you, and that difference will draw some but is most often misunderstood by many and attacked by others. Doing the right thing puts the spotlight on all who choose the path most traveled—the path of least resistance—the path you rejected. Some will follow; others will even resent your love. Love and forgiveness undeserved burns as hot coals on the head of the one refusing to admit the need for either.

These verses are from the beatitudes as recorded by Matthew. Beatitude means ultimate blessedness or bliss. "Blessed," according to the Hebrew from which this is derived, is about an internal impact on your heart (joy, peace, happiness, hope). It is not anything external that God is to do for you or what you are to do for others, but something that happens TO you, from the inside, when you have a heart that is right with God. Even persecution by others deeply touches your spirit, and it either draws you into the comforting arms of your Savior or seeks comfort in denial.

You may not have looked at your decision quite as logically as the steps outlined above, but that's what happened. Now as you mature, you walk back through those steps over and over, understanding your need for God, choosing to turn to him or away, finding freedom, and growing enough to offer that same gift to others. It's a wonderful journey if you consider it is never complete, so you must enjoy the path.

BOTTOM LINE

A lot of people choose not to trust in Jesus because they believe that once they have made the choice to accept him the journey is over and they stop growing. Nothing could be further from the truth. Attaching yourself to Christ and walking as a brand-new person, you realize the world looks different; everything you thought you knew of what life should be like becomes new. Finally, it becomes true. Finally it becomes a life worth living to the fullest—a life full of new discovery of yourself, God, and the world around you every day. In many ways, it is as if you are a child and every turn is a brand-new discovery. Do you understand the impact of what God did for you? Now accept that your eternity with God has already begun. Live life to the fullest. Live a life of faith.

 ## TALK TO GOD:

This is a time for celebration. Just relax and enjoy God. Think about what you love about Jesus and tell him about it. Let him know your thoughts and feelings about this relationship you now share. Let him in on your hopes for the future.

 ## DIG DEEPER:

Read through Matthew 5:3–10 and write down your own personal experience with each of these "Blessings." How was your spirit poor? What did you mourn? When did you desire to be cleansed and made righteous? How were you shown mercy? Now go back through verses 7–9 and think about people God has brought into your path. How can you show them mercy, love them with a pure heart, and help them make peace with God? Now, will you choose to do it and truly live as Jesus did?

Now What?

You believed; now you read a book. Maybe you prayed some, maybe you prayed a lot. Maybe you studied a little, maybe you did every exercise suggested to dig deeper into understanding and grow in your relationship with God. Maybe you just skipped to the last chapter to see what the punch line is to help you decide if this book is worth reading.

I can't know the answers to these possibilities as I write these words. I do not have any idea what impact the characters and spaces grouped together on these pages may have on you. But there are a few things I do know about your situation, whether we will ever share a real conversation over e-mail, paper, air, or not.

There are truths about God that are true whether or not you choose to believe them, of which the most important is his desire for intimacy with you—for you to know you are desperately loved and to trust in his goodness, power, and mercy.

There are also truths about your role in that relationship that will also remain true regardless of your perspective—mainly, that your spiritual development is just as much up to you as it is up to God, but you will at times be too immature, selfish, dense, deaf, and blind to do anything but hurt yourself.

Nobody can mature you in any way, especially spiritually—

not church, mentors, pastors, teachers, authors, family, or friends. Nope, all maturity is about you walking toward the unknown. Spiritual maturity is about walking toward the unknown holding the hand of Jesus.

On this journey you will discover the truth of your character, most of the time, finding it in need; and that is precisely the beauty of the journey.

Not in the need, but in the supply—the supply of grace for failure, strength for weakness, love for loneliness, peace for fear. You will discover you are not alone, never really were, and if you remain aware, never will think otherwise. Because you can now see beyond yourself with the eyes of God, you will discover that you are capable of more than you are capable. You find yourself calmed with the sense of supernatural control over the seemingly uncontrollable. You become aware that life is not centered on you, but you are the reason for everything.

As your relationship with God unfolds, at first you find rest for your soul, then healing for your heart, and ultimately passion and love for others.

This book has attempted to provide some possible, not absolute, answers to questions you may face. Now you face more questions. What will you do with this new beginning? Where will you place your trust when you are tested? Where will you choose to rest your hope?

God invites you to continue your life hoping and trusting in him.

You believed, now what?

That's the question you have to answer. It ain't in this book. It's in yours. What will you allow God to write?

About the Author

"My Window of Calling"

Was there a window to your soul in your youth—something that allowed a breeze of a message from God to guide and instruct you? What made you truly happy? What memory sticks out as a defining moment in your childhood that began the recurring connection of joy throughout your adult life?

What is the thing you lose track of time doing? What is your calling?

The latter is a question I have asked of my own life, at times, obsessively. I've counseled people wrestling with this question to dig deep into the thing that time has no hold of— the place where the laws of sleep deprivation, schedule, and responsibility all fall away when you are in its throes. Most stare at me as if I'm an alien, or worse yet, right.

Most people feel that doing the thing they love to do is selfish, inconsiderate, irresponsible, and too good to be true. Most people who feel this way live with questions of lives not lived, of what could have been, of regret. Our lives we do not choose, but our response to life is all about free will. God allows us to choose our actions, not our circumstances.

Mankind, though, desires to manipulate the uncontrollable, and we lose track of what we truly can have dominion over.

God desires us to fulfill our destiny. He has a calling for each of us. Is that what you will make your living doing? I don't know. Is it something that you should spend considerable effort figuring out? Absolutely.

There were a few windows to my soul's calling as a child. The most significant was a homework assignment in fourth grade at Reese Road Elementary School in Columbus, Georgia, where I spent much of my youth. We were to write a made-up story, include pictures, design a cover, laminate it, and bind the book as if it were heading to the local bookstore.

I struggled for inspiration. It wasn't the project or the grade that drove me—it was the vision, the inspiration, finding the perfect angle. No basic story of horses or knights would have sufficed. There must be mystery and surprise. It must be intelligent, and most of all, the reader must learn something.

My inspiration came one day while watching Saturday-morning cartoons. It was Tarzan, I believe, and the lesson that day, the thing I walked away with, was a scientific fact I was assured none of my classmates would know. I had my story, a mystery with a twist. The character would be Shermie (short for Sherman), a bespectacled, freckled, shy, smart, bookworm of a little boy, who begins the story not too popular. But after saving the day with his wits, Shermie is revered as a hero. Unbeknownst to the writer at the time, Shermie was me, or at least the me I knew in my fantasies.

The details of the story elude me now, as the book is long since lost, but the gist was a detective-like quest for the

"Mother of all Diamonds." Danger, bad guys, and a puppy companion peppered the words and pictures. Everyone was in the hunt for this incredible diamond, thought to be larger than any ever beheld. It was true, although a million years and millions of tons of pressure too early. It was a lump of coal. A sizable lump, but coal nonetheless. I was amazed that simple coal under such great pressure over such long periods of time could create a priceless diamond. I was certain everyone else would be amazed, too. My storyline was sure to be a hit.

Shermie solved the mystery, and everybody learned something.

I spent countless hours writing and rewriting that story in my mind. Time was irrelevant. Playing outside or even watching TV took an easy second fiddle. I was obsessed. I saw not only a story, but a cartoon series, and Hardy Boys-like novels of Shermie traveling the world solving mysteries. There would be "Shermie and the Mystery of whatever" lunch boxes, posters, and movies. I was strategizing and marketing a product that didn't yet exist, a skill that would unintentionally serve me well during the Internet boom of the 1990s.

God has built upon that moment countless times, but until I had enough pieces, until I was in the midst of that calling, I never saw the puzzle for what it was. Was that glimpse into my soul a trigger leading me to be a writer? No, I think not. I heard in a writing seminar once, that there are two kinds of writers: one will write his entire life regardless of ever publishing, the other has something specific to say to a particular audience and chooses to write because it is the best forum to communicate that message. I am a writer of the latter sort.

Just as today the shelves are rife with the works of men and women more gifted in prose than I, there were even better writers in my fourth grade class and better product produced. But nobody else made the reader look at something common in a different way. See, that is the glimpse into my soul's calling. It's always the moment that resonates, that lingers in the air of my memory as the smell of something perfect in purpose.

This glimpse occurred many more times throughout my youth, from building robots out of old car parts to piecing together sound systems for rock concerts. It wasn't that I liked making things, I just liked making common things find purpose in new ways. I loved taking piece parts that didn't naturally belong together, making something new and functional, and teaching others who were interested how it all worked.

It happened again my senior year in high school in Mrs. Clark's English class. She was the kind of teacher that only referred to students in their formal name—Mr. Simpson, Miss Schiavone. I mean, really, did anyone speak that way? She was a cold, calloused old woman with the makeup of the walking dead, a tight brown bun, and those beady little eyes whose soul-sapping laser beams were held back only by the horn rimmed reading glasses at the tip of her nose. At least that's how most of us incorrectly saw her. I began to see her differently, though, as these windows to my soul began to open through her touch on my life.

I never did my studies outside of class, and never learned how to prepare in advance. School wasn't much of a challenge in my early youth, and by the time it was, I had lost interest in the perfect grade point average. Once when interpreting a poem, Mrs. Clark keenly observed I was furiously reading while the first person called upon was relaying their perspective. She quickly called on me as I was finishing the last stanza. I believe I even made her wait a moment before I responded, so that I could finish the final line.

Abruptly, I gave my interpretation, awaiting the verbal whack across the ego; but much to my horror, there was no comment at all. She stared at me, paused a moment, turned, and headed back to her desk. Everyone held his or her breath. Some looked at me and grimaced, shaking their heads in knowing empathy of what was inevitably to arrive. I had done it now. She not only was angry, she was too angry to speak. I was done for.

Then as quickly as the noose had been placed around my neck, she moved on to the next segment of our lesson. She never even acknowledged I had spoken a single word.

The next day, almost all had been forgotten, though a tiny twinge of fear grabbed hold of the hairs on my neck as soon as English class began. Mrs. Clark stood in front of us and spoke words that surprised us. To this day, her words have helped define my life. She said, "Yesterday, Michael …"

Michael? Every head and eye in the class immediately jerked in my direction.

I wasn't Michael, I was Mr. Simpson. Why was I suddenly Michael?

This can't be good. I dripped through the cracks in my chair—fresh meat being prepared for dinner with the Big Bad Wolf.

She continued, "Yesterday, Michael gave an interpretation

of the poem we were studying that I have never heard. I looked through all my books and then spent some time last evening in the college library searching for any interpretation that had a similar perspective, but came up empty. I believe Michael may have been correct."

Michael may have been correct?

Michael had never thought about what he was saying before he said it. Michael had never read that poem until that very moment. Michael was, as usual, winging it.

Something, though, something of truth burst forth from my soul at that moment. The moment I spoke what I felt without thinking and the moment I saw the impact on others when I helped them look at something familiar—something seemingly common—in a fresh way; that was the moment God spoke to me.

That moment—the moment I knew that an uncommon perspective was not only acceptable, it was beneficial—lingered for years and often surfaced in interesting ways. The gift of helping others see the familiar with new eyes defined my professional career and catapulted me from an inexperienced, relatively uneducated, sales engineer to helping define and engineer the turn-around strategy for a two billon dollar software company.

It led me to become the Chief Marketing Officer for a burgeoning corporation and led me out of the corporate world and into writing when the last strategy I contributed to was to sell that same company, saving our shareholders millions by preempting the crash of the tech market. It leads me regularly to counsel CEOs, presidents, and marketing professionals in companies of all sizes on strategies for their future. Weekly, it allows me to help new Christians and those yet to savor the taste of grace look at God in new ways.

It is why I think out loud. It is why I speak. It is why I am writing this book.

Once I saw her true self, Mrs. Clark was no longer a mean old hag of a professor. She was actually an attractive but unassuming woman who so dearly respected and hoped for the future of her students that she pushed them to whatever greatness they could glimpse while within her influence. She was a gifted teacher who opened possibilities of life through the words of the great writers of old, and helped young people see past the false realities of life's self-imposed limitations to a land of promise awakened by their own minds.

In that senior high English class, I awakened to the reality of who she truly was, as well as who I could become. Although I repressed that glimpse more often than not in the next ten years, that memory lingered. That smell of perfect purpose wafted through the air of my memory and one year after meeting Christ heart to heart, became startlingly pungent to the point of stirring me from the safety of the comfortable and catapulted me into a quest for fulfilling my purpose.

I had always seen differently, but rarely spoke of my thoughts, preferring to stew in them and seethe with angst. I decided one day that God had gifted me with a mind holding unique perspectives, and I should value it over comfort or risk spitting in the face of the giver. I vowed to not shy from the opportunity to express an unpopular point of view, always with the intention of doing the right thing even if it hurt me. Jesus and the apostle Paul were my guides and inspiration.

Opportunity abounded and although the maturity of discretion came later, the die was cast. I was branded by half the company as savior and the other half as Satan. I was a somewhat reluctant agent of change in a culture of desperation; the perfect breeding ground for unformed ideas. The corporate world was my playground and the little child, the author of a silly little story about a lump of coal, was released into the world with reckless abandon.

My life and the lives of those around me will never be the same.

What is your glimpse into perfect purpose? You've had one, probably many. What is the essence of the unique thing you provide to the world? It isn't what you "do," it's who you "are" and what you were created to be. What you do will constantly change, sometimes quite radically, but what you are will only evolve once you allow Christ into your center. You are pure in God's eyes and perfectly loved as his son or daughter. You have the power of the Creator of the Universe at your disposal. What will you do with it? What will you allow him to do through you?

Notes

1 From the movie *Shrek*, ® and © 2001 DreamWorks LLC.
2 *U.S. News and World Report*, May 6, 2002, "Faith in America" pp. 42–43; *Religion and Ethics Newsweekly/U.S. News and World Report* poll of 2002 adults conducted by Milofsky International and Edison Media Research, March 26–April 4, 2002.
3 A. W. Tozer, *The Knowledge of the Holy* (HarperCollins: NY, 1961), p. 1.
4 Ibid. p. 2 paraphrase of last sentence, paragraph 6.
5 Michael L. Simpson in *Permission Evangelism* (NexGen: Colorado Springs, Colo., 2003), pp. 141–142.

ABOUT THE AUTHOR

Michael Simpson, award-winning author, is a recognized speaker in over twenty countries. When he is not writing or personally discipling young believers, he travels throughout Eastern Europe, Western Europe, and North America inspiring Christians to pursue God's passion for their life. He is available to help you and the people of your organization experience God in new ways through talks and workshops at churches, retreats, and conferences. His ground-breaking insights published in the book *Permission Evangelism: When to Talk, When to Walk* (Cook, 2003), was awarded the prestigious Gold Medallion Award for Excellence in Evangelism Literature.

Since 1992, Michael has been involved in many aspects of ministry, from church plants and re-architecting existing organizations, to co-leading a para-church outreach non-profit. This experience coupled with his sixteen years in business strategy and consulting and years meeting with pastors and church leaders as a speaker/consultant, has helped him develop insights for inspiring believers as a dynamic speaker. Michael Simpson is available to speak on topics regarding evangelism, post-modern ministry, modern-day discipleship, and futures of ministry. Some popular presentations include "Enabling Hearts of Evangelism," "Making Disciples in a Post-Christian World," and "Growing Your Intimacy with God by Sharing Your Faith."

Contact info@permissionevangelism.com to determine if a partnership would be beneficial for your organization.

See what others are saying:

"Michael spoke several times at our church retreat. The reaction of our church family was amazing! Virtually every person who attended sought me out and thanked me for selecting Michael as our speaker for the retreat. Many found that reviewing their own story of conversion in light of these principles shed new light on their relationship with Christ. This was the most practical and useful evangelism training we have ever had."

"Michael did an incredible job of empowering me, refreshing my spirit, and fanning my heart for the lost. His practical "tips" really encouraged me to go to the next level with my non-believing friends. Thanks!"

"Great! Very practical!"

"Excellent. Surprisingly logical but very original and cutting edge."

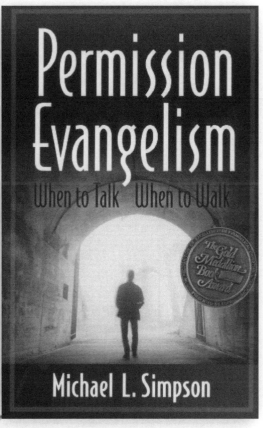

The Word at Work Around the World

A vital part of Cook Communications Ministries is our international outreach, Cook Communications Ministries International (CCMI). Your purchase of this book, and of other books and Christian-growth products from Cook, enables CCMI to provide Bibles and Christian literature to people in more than 150 languages in 65 countries.

Cook Communications Ministries is a not-for-profit, self-supporting organization. Revenues from sales of our books, Bible curricula, and other church and home products not only fund our U.S. ministry, but also fund our CCMI ministry around the world. One hundred percent of donations to CCMI go to our international literature programs.

CCMI reaches out internationally in three ways:

• Our premier International Christian Publishing Institute (ICPI) trains leaders from nationally led publishing houses around the world.

• We provide literature for pastors, evangelists, and Christian workers in their national language.

• We reach people at risk—refugees, AIDS victims, street children, and famine victims—with God's Word.

Word Power, God's Power

Faith Kidz, RiverOak, Honor, Life Journey, Victor, NexGen — every time you purchase a book produced by Cook Communications Ministries, you not only meet a vital personal need in your life or in the life of someone you love, but you're also a part of ministering to José in Colombia, Humberto in Chile, Gousa in India, or Lidiane in Brazil. You help make it possible for a pastor in China, a child in Peru, or a mother in West Africa to enjoy a life-changing book. And because you helped, children and adults around the world are learning God's Word and walking in his ways.

Thank you for your partnership in helping to disciple the world. May God bless you with the power of his Word in your life.

For more information about our international ministries, visit www.ccmi.org.

Additional copies of *I Believe, Now What?*
and other NexGen titles are available
from your local bookseller.

If you have enjoyed this book,
or if it has had an impact on your life,
we would like to hear from you.

Please contact us at:

NexGen Books
Cook Communications Ministries, Dept. 201
4050 Lee Vance View
Colorado Springs, CO 80918

Or visit our Web site: www.cookministries.com

NEXGEN®

Building the New Generation of Believers